LET'S GET BACK TO BASICS:

PRAYER

Paul M. Bromfield

DEDICATION

I dedicate this book to every believer in Christ who seeks to deepen their understanding of prayer.

I also dedicate this book to those who set the example in my Christian Walk, showing that prayer was not an option but a mandatory part of my faith.

ACKNOWLEDGMENTS

I would like to acknowledge Dr. Phyllis Bromfield, my mother, who encouraged me to pursue my doctorate in theology, which helped give birth to this book.

FOREWORD

Let's Get Back to Basics - Prayer is a book that's needed in a time of artificial intelligence, doctrines of devils, and fast modern technology. *Luke 18:1* says, *"That men ought to always pray."* Prayer is the lifeline of the believer. Prayer brings clarity and direction, divinely connecting us directly with God. *Matthew 21:13* declares, *"My house will be called a house of prayer."* Jesus identifies the house of God as a praying house.

Let's Get Back to Basics - Prayer delivers the blueprint for the Body of Christ to get back to making the house of God and our personal lives centered on what Jesus centered His Kingdom on: prayer.

Apostle Dion Nesmith,
Voice of The Dove, Queens, New York

TABLE OF CONTENTS

INTRODUCTION:
LET'S GET BACK TO BASICS, THE SERIES

When I say "Back to Basics," I'm not talking about something elementary or watered down. I know that some may hear the word "basic" and think, "There's nothing basic about my Jesus or my relationship with God," and you're absolutely right. There's nothing ordinary about Him. However, when I speak of basic, I mean what is foundational and essential. The things you can't leave out if you want to grow strong in your faith.

Think of it like baking. Recipes have measurements for a reason. If you skip a key ingredient—or add too much or too little—the whole cake can collapse. In the same way, if a believer doesn't have the right spiritual ingredients, they won't become all that God intended them to be.

That's what this *Let's Get Back to Basics* series is all about: helping Christians—whether new in the faith or seasoned in ministry—make sure their foundation is solid. These books are written for individuals who have been in church for years but have never received in-depth teaching on core truths. They're also for those who are just coming into the body of Christ, trying to figure out what this walk really entails.

I thank God for churches that offer classes for new members. That's a great start. However, in my experience, there are certain subjects—such as prayer, fasting, and others—that often don't receive the attention they deserve. Sometimes leaders assume people already know these things. Other times, people copy what they've seen without truly understanding it.

Some readers may come from different denominations with completely different spiritual practices. Let's be real—a Catholic mass and a Pentecostal service are two very different experiences. If no one ever breaks things down, it's easy to feel lost, or worse, disconnected.

That's why I wrote this book and this series. My heart is to help bridge the gap between seeing with your eyes and knowing in your spirit, between religious activity and relational understanding.

Whether you've been saved five days or fifty years, we all need to learn and even return to the foundational truths of our faith—and build from there. *Let's Get Back to Basics.*

INTRODUCTION: *PRAYER*

In every generation, God's people have had to reclaim what was lost—not by chasing after something new, but by returning to something ancient, something sacred, something foundational. That's what this book is about.

In a world filled with spiritual shortcuts and rapid innovation, it's easy to lose touch with the very heartbeat of our faith: *prayer*. We've learned how to host dynamic services, launch ministries, and build platforms—but somewhere along the way, many have quietly let go of the most essential gift God gave us: the ministry of prayer.

And I don't mean surface-level, routine prayer. I'm not talking about the kind you perform in public for applause, or the kind you only pull out in emergencies. I'm not even talking about the prayer that rushes in with a list of demands, then rushes back out without waiting for God to respond.

I'm talking about real prayer—the kind that shifts atmospheres. The kind that moves heaven and transforms the earth. The kind of prayer that deepens intimacy with The Father, strengthens your spirit, and aligns you with the will of God.

This book is not for perfect prayer warriors—it's for real people. It's for the believer who's ever whispered, "Am I doing this right?" It's for the one who says grace over food but struggles to go deeper. It's for the seasoned saint who's grown a little rusty and the new Christian who's just discovering that prayer is more than memorized lines.

Wherever you are on the journey, this book is for you, because prayer isn't a luxury—it's a necessity. It's the oxygen of the believer's life. You can't thrive in your walk with God without it. You can't discern truth, resist temptation, or fulfill your purpose without it.

This book isn't a book of lofty theology or mystical formulas. It's a return to the fundamentals of prayer—solid biblical truth, practical insight, and Spirit-led instruction. Just like a strong building needs a firm foundation, your walk with God requires a deep and consistent prayer life.

Together, we'll explore types of prayer, the biblical model of prayer, heart posture, persistence, and praying with authority. Furthermore, we'll explore how to intercede for others, how to hear from God, and even confront misconceptions.

For some Christians, prayer has become a performance. For others, a vending machine, where they feel like they can put a prayer in to purchase and receive what they want. Then for far too many, after they've prayed and prayed for a long time, seemingly their prayers going unanswered, they left from praying.

I believe God sent me to help you rekindle your passion for prayer and to show you that prayer isn't about having the right words—it's about having the right heart. It's not about public display—it's about private surrender. So let's begin again. Let's unlearn religion and rediscover relationship. Let's close the door, kneel in the secret place, and open our hearts again. Let's get back to real prayer. Let's get back to powerful prayer. Let's get back to biblical prayer. *Let's Get Back to Basics: Prayer.*

CHAPTER 1:
PRAYER 101

As I wrote in the introduction—and I feel it is necessary to repeat for emphasis here—when I speak of *back to basics,* I don't in any way diminish what prayer is; instead, I speak of *basic,* meaning it is foundational. I will lay some groundwork for what needs to be understood about prayer as an established individual in this Christian Walk.

In the times we are living in, prayer is essential like never before. I believe a life of prayer is a must for all who believe in God. I aim to demystify prayer in the eyes of people who feel they can't fathom how to pray like other dedicated Christians do. People will see others praying earnestly in a church service, on Facebook Live, or in another virtual setting, and they may never imagine themselves doing the same. Reaching the point of praying with such comfort begins with a solid foundation. Let us begin this journey.

What is Prayer?

Let us discuss what prayer is. The most straightforward definition is this: It is a two-way communication with The Father. You likely have prayed and given God a list of things you desired. You may have told Him how you felt about a matter, asked for forgiveness for some wrong you committed, or something else, and then said *Amen.* Based on the definition

I shared with you, ask yourself, "Did I really engage in the essence of true prayer?" If you can be honest with yourself, what you had was a one-sided conversation with God.

When you truly pray, you allow God the space to speak back to you. You may have rushed out of your one-sided conversation with God while He was waiting to give you the answer to your question or respond to you. He was waiting to provide you with a *spiritual download* or clarity, offering new insights from His Word. However, after you expressed what you wanted, you then decided to pursue other things.

From now on, I challenge you to stop that narrative. There will be times when you have a brief prayer, perhaps when you wake up in the morning, and you thank The Father for another day, for life and strength, and request protection throughout the day. You may even cry out, "Help me, Lord," when you encounter a problematic situation in your day. But I challenge you to set aside time to pray. Don't short-change God. God desires to spend time with you. He wants to speak back to you just as you talked to Him. *God is a listening God. Also*, He is a speaking God, unlike other gods of this world who do not speak.

The Posture of Prayer

There is a posture to prayer. Many of you are likely familiar with the practice of standing while praying. Yet, I want to shine light on the term posture. By posture, I'm not referring to the position or how you stand or kneel while praying. Instead, I'm referring to the posture of your heart.

Do you take prayer as an inconvenience or a disruption to your day? Do you drag yourself to the bedside to pray when you really want to go to sleep instead? Do you put prayer as the last thing on your list—the bottom of the things you need to take care of? Also, do you go into prayer expecting God to be your personal genie, where your wish is His command? Do you only pray when you need something? Do you only pray when you are in a jam or some type of trouble?

I need you to really reflect on these questions. If someone only called me when they needed something, I would feel like I was being used or taken advantage of. Am I not good enough for more than just your requests? Am I not good enough to speak to you outside of your emergency? It is amazing how we will try to use God for what we want. Then, discard Him after we get it—until the next time.

Also, what is your mindset going into prayer? You should never think that you can ever manipulate God because He knows the true desires of your heart. I would like you to think about the fact that when God only hears from you when you want something, you have gone into prayer with an ulterior motive or agenda. You only want what He can give you and not Him. You only want what He can offer you. You only want what He has in His hand. Instead, pray with the mindset that it's not about what you can get out of it, but how much deeper your relationship will grow as you spend time with Him. Again, posture is not about standing, kneeling, or prostrating on the floor. It's about the posture of our heart.

Who to Pray For?

Who should we pray for? Should we pray only for ourselves and our loved ones, or also for others? Should prayer only be for our friends and acquaintances who have our support? Absolutely not. Our prayers can't be selfish but selfless. *1 Timothy 2:1 (AMP)* says, *"First of all, then, I urge that petitions (specific requests), prayers, intercessions (prayers for others), and thanksgivings be offered on behalf of all people."* Paul used a tiny but defining word: *"all."* Our family, friends, enemies, government, nations, city, unbelievers, believers, spiritual leaders, and churches can be covered anytime we pray.

You may say, "Wait a minute, you put on the list of people my enemies?" I know it may be a hard thing to do, but The Word of The Lord says in *Matthew 5:44 (AMP)*, *"But I say to you, love [that is, unselfishly seek the best or higher good for] your enemies and pray for those who persecute you."* This action is the Christian way. Even though you may know people who don't mean the best for you, The Word of The Lord says to pray. This action shows a level of spiritual maturity.

And another thing, please don't pray for your enemy's demise; Jesus wasn't speaking to that. Your prayer should never be, "Lord, kill my enemy" or "Lord, do to them what they did to me." That is not the Christian way. There are principles in The Bible that speak to the heart of those who are evil, such as reaping and sowing. *Proverbs 22:8 (AMP)* says, *"He who sows injustice will reap [a harvest of] trouble."*

So, when we pray, we don't put limits on love. We pray beyond our own circle—beyond convenience—and we let our prayers reflect the heart of God: covering "all," even when it's hard, and trusting God to handle what's unjust.

Who to Pray With?

James 5:16 (AMP)

"Therefore, confess your sins to one another [your false steps, your offenses], and pray for one another, that you may be healed and restored. The heartfelt and persistent prayer of a righteous man (believer) can accomplish much [when put into action and made effective by God—it is dynamic and can have tremendous power]."

Paul said, "Pray for one another." That picks up everyone, including believers. Yet, James discusses how believers should take one another's prayers to The Lord. Christians are to confess their sins, false steps, or offenses to one another. Only those who have a heart for God can do this.

Here's something to note: Please don't think that just because an individual worships in your church, they have a loving heart. It's a hard pill to swallow, but it is real. Not everyone is Christlike in character in the house of God. So, an individual you can truly confide in should be the one you go to. Why would you confide in them? Because it helps with accountability. It also doesn't make you feel you must deal with the struggle alone.

Pray for and with one another, as it aids in your healing (and theirs) from emotional scars—guilt, shame, and offenses—and ultimately results in restoration.

You may have heard of a term like a *"prayer partner."* It's not a glorified term just to say that individuals pray together; it denotes that strength is exchanged as they pray for one another. According to scripture, prayer is effective and powerful, especially when you have a prayer partner.

When to Pray?

What does The Bible say about when to pray?

Psalm 63:1 (KJV)

> *"O God, thou art my God; early will I seek thee: my soul thirsteth for thee, my flesh longeth for thee in a dry and thirsty land, where no water is."*

The psalmist here has decided to seek The Lord early and make that their specific time to spend with Him.

Psalm 5:3 (AMP)

"In the morning, O Lord, You will hear my voice; in the morning I will prepare [a prayer and a sacrifice] for You and watch and wait [for You to speak to my heart]."

The psalmist again speaks of morning prayer.

I believe we should all acknowledge The Lord for another day and speak to The Father before going about our day at work, school, etc. The psalmist in Psalm 5:3 has such a surety that when he makes time to pray, God will speak to his heart. He waits for God to speak to his heart, which lets me know he is spending real time with The Father. It was more than just talking to The Father to begin his day. The psalmist in this verse has committed to spending real time in prayer with The Lord in the morning. By the way, in both passages, David is the credited author of the psalm.

Luke 18:1 (AMP)

"Now Jesus was telling the disciples a parable to make the point that at all times they ought to pray and not give up and lose heart."

Jesus clearly states that we should pray at all times and not give up praying or lose heart because we don't get the answer to our prayers—keep on praying.

Ephesians 6:18 (AMP)

"With all prayer and petition pray [with specific requests] at all times [on every occasion and in every season] in The Spirit, and with this in view, stay alert with all perseverance and petition [interceding in prayer] for all God's people."

1 Thessalonians 5:17 (AMP)

"Be unceasing and persistent in prayer."

Please note that these scriptures do not refer to an individual praying 24 hours a day, every day, for 365 days. Rather, they refer to a person who leaves the line of communication open to The Lord. You can pray in your car, at work, or walking on the street—any time of the day, night, evening, or afternoon. The Lord wants us to have a praying spirit.

Sometimes, God will specifically instruct you, saying, "I want to meet you every morning at 5 a.m." If this prompting comes from The Lord, ensure you show up at that specific time every day.

I believe many may have missed a Word from God because God set a time, and they were late or didn't show up at all. God may just have you do this for a season, but listen to His voice if it happens. There is a blessing in your obedience.

So, when should you pray? The answer is simple: pray continually, consistently, and with intentionality. Whether it's in the quiet of the morning, the middle of your day, or a prompting in the night, prayer is never confined to a clock. God desires a relationship, not a ritual. The key is to remain sensitive to His voice and willing to respond—because the more time you spend with The Father, the more you'll realize: there's never a wrong time to pray.

Where to Pray?

Where should we pray? Anywhere. I used to have a mindset that when I wanted to spend time with God, I had to put on my music, create the proper atmosphere, get a pillow to kneel on, and then pray to The Father, which was my physical posture before I could pray. Prayer wasn't prayer until I did that. Over time, I realized it wasn't about a particular place but that I was uninterrupted and committed to that time of prayer, regardless of the location.

Years ago, I watched a famous preacher on television say he prayed in the shower. At the time, this blew my mind because it wasn't something I had done before, but I can see how it could work for those who claim they don't have time or live in a house filled with kids. A longer shower and fellowship with The Lord may be ideal for them.

Let's take a look at some places where people prayed.

- *Jonah 2:1 (AMP)* says, *"Then Jonah prayed to The Lord his God from the stomach of the fish."* Jonah prayed in the belly of a great fish, and God heard him. As long as you are living, there is nowhere on earth you can't pray that God won't hear your voice.

- *Lamentations 3:55 (AMP)* says, *"I called on Your name, O Lord, out of the lowest pit."* The Lord can still hear you even in the lowest pit—literal or figurative.

- *Matthew 26:36 (AMP)* says, *"Then Jesus came with them to a place called Gethsemane (olive-press), and He told His disciples, 'Sit here while I go over there and pray.'"* Jesus went to a garden to pray.

- *Mark 6:46 (AMP)* says, *"After He said goodbye to them, He went to the mountain to pray."* Jesus would often leave His disciples to go to the mountains to pray.

- *Luke 2:37 (AMP)* says, *"And then [there was] a widow to the age of eighty-four. She did not leave the [area of the] temple but was serving and worshiping night and day with fastings and prayers."* This woman of God prayed in the temple day and night, even into her old age.

- *Luke 5:16 (AMP) says, "But Jesus Himself would often slip away to the wilderness and pray [in seclusion]."* Jesus would also pray in the wilderness.

- *Acts 10:9 (AMP) says, "The next day, as they were on their way and were approaching the city, Peter went up on the roof of the house about the sixth hour (noon) to pray."* Peter changed it up from praying in the house to praying on the roof.

- *Acts 21:5 (AMP) says, "When our days there came to an end, we left and proceeded on our journey, while all of the disciples, with their wives and children, escorted us on our way until we were outside the city. After kneeling down on the beach and praying, we told one another goodbye."* The people of God prayed at an unconventional place—the beach. We often think of the beach as a place of recreation. Why not a place to pray as well?

These scriptures demonstrate that prayer is not confined to a specific location.

Chapter Reflection and Activation

1. When you reflect on your current prayer life, do you view it as a conversation with God or a monologue? What has shaped that perspective?

2. What time in your day or week can you dedicate to uninterrupted prayer, and what would help you protect that time consistently?

3. In what ways has your heart posture toward prayer been shaped by routine, convenience, or desperation? How can you begin to approach God with more sincerity and intentionality?

4. After praying, how often do you pause to listen for God's response? What can you do to make space for hearing Him more clearly?

Now that we've laid the foundation of what prayer truly is—a personal, ongoing relationship with God—it's time to look deeper. Prayer isn't just one thing. Just like communication takes many forms, so does prayer. In the next chapter, we'll explore the different types of prayer God has given us so you can learn how—and when—to use them.

CHAPTER 2:
DIFFERENT TYPES OF PRAYER

You may or may not know, but we can find different types of prayers spoken of in The Word of The Lord. Let's examine the following types of prayer: the prayer of faith, the prayer of agreement (also known as corporate prayer), the prayer of request, petition, or supplication, the prayer of thanksgiving, the prayer of worship, the prayer of consecration, and the prayer of intercession.

The Prayer of Faith

James 5:14-15 (AMP)

"14 Is anyone among you sick? He must call for the elders (spiritual leaders) of the church and they are to pray over him, anointing him with oil in the name of The Lord; 15 and the prayer of faith will restore the one who is sick, and The Lord will raise him up; and if he has committed sins, he will be forgiven."

We see several elements taking place in this scripture. James declares here that the elders, *the ecclesia*, are to be called for those who are sick. James says they are to anoint the individual with oil and lay hands on that individual. Next, James says that they are to pray for them "in the name of The Lord." You may hear people pray and say the words "in the name of Jesus" either within or at the end of their prayer. This statement is not just something done out of tradition but is rooted in The Word of The Lord, as noted in verse 14.

Lastly, James follows up in verse 15 by saying that the prayer of faith will restore them, raise them up, and their sins will be forgiven. This verse speaks to the power of prayer, specifically a prayer done by the elders in faith.

The prayer of faith is for physical, spiritual, and mental healing, where restoration will come to an individual's life. God desires to do an overhaul in the lives of believers, so when the prayer of faith occurs, transformation takes place.

The Prayer of Agreement or Corporate Prayer

Acts 2:42 (AMP)

"They were continually and faithfully devoting themselves to the instruction of the apostles, and to fellowship, to eating meals together and to prayers."

This scripture specifies the coming together of a people in one accord to pray. When we hear the term "corporate prayer," there are sometimes misconceptions. I once heard on Instagram Live where a viewer asked if corporate prayer was when you prayed for businesses, which highlights why teaching like this is necessary—to clear up misunderstandings. Corporate prayer is not about praying for one's business.

Acts 12:5 (AMP)

> *"So Peter was kept in prison, but fervent and persistent prayer for him was being made to God by the church."*

In Acts 12:5, people came together, praying for a specific purpose. The result of this prayer is seen in *Acts 12:11 (AMP)*: *"When Peter came to his senses, he said, 'Now I know for certain that The Lord has sent His angel and has rescued me from the hand of Herod and from all that the Jewish people were expecting [to do to me].'"* There is power in corporate prayer when people decide to come together to pray.

In a church service, you may see one individual praying, and those in attendance should agree with that person leading prayer by praising, worshipping, making declarations, repeating what they said, or simply saying "Amen," "Thank you, God," or "Yes, Lord."

This practice of agreeing in prayer is not just religious—it's biblical.

- In Deuteronomy 27, the people responded with "Amen" after each declaration of God's law, affirming their alignment with His truth.

- In Matthew 18:19, where Jesus says, *"If two of you shall agree on earth as touching anything that they shall ask, it shall be done for them of My Father which is in Heaven."* Agreement matters.

- In 2 Corinthians 1:20, Paul writes, *"For all the promises of God in Him are yea, and in Him Amen, unto the glory of God by us."* That "Amen" is not a ritual ending; it's a declaration of agreement with what was spoken.

We have seen scriptural examples where agreement matters. Whether it's a quiet "Yes, Lord" or a bold declaration, these responses demonstrate unity in faith—and unity is the place where God commands the blessing (Psalm 133:1–3). Let's not pray over each other when we come together, but let's pray in agreement and corporately, as one leads the prayer.

Acts 1:12-14 (AMP)

"12 Then the disciples returned to Jerusalem from the mount called Olivet (Olive Grove), which is near Jerusalem, [only] a Sabbath day's journey (less than one mile) away. 13 When they had entered the city, they went upstairs to the upper room where they were staying [indefinitely]; that is, Peter, and John and [his brother] James, and Andrew, Philip and Thomas, Bartholomew (Nathanael) and Matthew, James the son of Alphaeus, and Simon the Zealot, and Judas (Thaddaeus) the son of James. 14 All these with one mind and one purpose were continually devoting themselves to prayer, [waiting together] along with the women, and Mary the mother of Jesus, and with His brothers.

"¹ When the day of Pentecost had come, they were all together in one place, ² and suddenly a sound came from heaven like a rushing violent wind, and it filled the whole house where they were sitting."

In these texts, we see that the disciples and some 120 people went to the upper room in Jerusalem and continually devoted themselves to prayer. Jesus told them to wait until The Holy Spirit came, as recorded in Acts 1:4. In Acts 2, we see the result of coming together in corporate prayer as a continued effort: *"...And suddenly there came a sound from heaven as of a rushing mighty wind..."* (Acts 2:2a, KJV).

Have we moved away from these services where we come together for corporate prayer? Do we relegate corporate prayer to 5 to 10 minutes just before service starts? Do we only come together in crisis? We need to return to having a church that prays together. In this age of technology, it is easier than ever to connect on a Zoom or conference phone line and pray.

Corporate prayer is not outdated—it's essential. When we gather with one mind and one purpose, just like the early church, Heaven responds. Whether in person or virtually, unity in prayer brings supernatural results. If we want to see revival, breakthrough, and fresh fire in our churches, it won't happen by accident. It starts with coming together—on purpose—to pray.

The Prayer of Request, Petition, or Supplication

This type of prayer involves sincerely asking, beseeching, or begging God for something earnestly and with all humility. Let me premise this by saying God is not asking you about your wildest dreams. For example, "Lord, give me a million dollars, a Lamborghini, a 5-million-dollar house." Wants and needs' are two different words. Besides, do prayer requests like these align with God's plan for your life? Can you afford the maintenance on an expensive home or car? If you get it, will you be able to keep it?

When people lift the prayer of request, they should ask for things in Scripture, things within their means, and things relevant to what is happening in their lives. Even when a request is outside of one's means, it should align with God's hand upon one's life, as God will then equip them to handle whatever is outside of their means. Let's pray and make our requests related to what is going on in our lives, rather than making requests based on what we see someone has on TV or social media, or some lustful desire.

Philippians 4:6 (AMP)

" Do not be anxious or worried about anything, but in everything [every circumstance and situation] by prayer and petition with thanksgiving, continue to make your [specific] requests known to God."

Paul encourages the church of Philippi to come before The Lord in every circumstance and situation. If you decide to pray, then you should not be gripped with anxiety and worry. By praying, you are saying to God, "I trust You with this thing that I am dealing with, and as I give it over to You, then I believe I don't have to fret about it any longer." How can you expect to receive answered prayers, overwhelmed with anxiety?

Every believer must know that nothing is too hard for God, and He won't be annoyed by your prayers or burdens. God wants you to come to Him. Aren't you glad God is not like man? Never think, "I don't want to bother God." "I don't want to be a nuisance." You don't have to worry about that with God. If you ever are, He will let you know that you no longer need to pray for that thing.

Let's further look at the prayer of request in The Scriptures:

1 Chronicles 21:8 (AMP)

"Then David said to God, 'I have sinned greatly because I have done this thing. But now, I beseech You, take away the wickedness and guilt of Your servant, for I have acted very foolishly.'"

David made this eager, earnest, personal request to The Lord. He wanted a change, not one that dealt with outward conditions, but an internal one. We don't only need to ask God for things, but also do as David did. We need to see what does not align with God's Word in our lives, be transparent before Him, and beseech Him for change.

Psalm 118:25 (AMP)

> *"O Lord, save now, we beseech You; O Lord, we beseech You, send now prosperity and give us success!"*

In this verse, we see another example of a prayer of request. The psalmist is asking for prosperity and success. Don't think you can't make a personal request for material things, such as a promotion on the job, for your business to be successful and for you to be financially stable. Being saved doesn't mean you have to be destitute. You can love The Lord, pray, and be a success in life. The key is to make it known to The Lord, and if it's His will and in alignment with His plan for you, then it will be done.

So, go ahead and ask—but ask with humility, with faith, and with purpose. Bring your specific needs before The Father, knowing He delights in hearing from His children. Whether it's provision, healing, clarity, or internal transformation, the key is to make your request known and trust Him with the outcome. God is not offended by your need—He's honored by your dependence.

The Prayer of Thanksgiving

Why should we give thanks? *1 Chronicles 16:34 (AMP)* says, *"O give thanks to The Lord, for He is good; for His lovingkindness endures forever."* The prayer of thanksgiving expresses gratitude for all God has done—and all He continues to do, even when we don't realize it.

When you wake up in the morning, tell The Lord, "Thank You." When He allows you to get home safely, tell Him, "Thank You." When your children return home without incident, or when your body feels stronger than the day before—give thanks. These may seem like small things, but gratitude for the daily mercies opens your eyes to just how much God is doing.

Thanksgiving is not just a good habit; it's a command. *1 Thessalonians 5:18* says, *"In everything give thanks: for this is the will of God in Christ Jesus concerning you."* It's not just about giving thanks *for* all things, but giving thanks *in* all things. Even in trials, God is worthy of praise.

The prayer of thanksgiving also shapes the posture of your heart. It prepares you to become the type of worshiper God desires—those who worship Him in spirit and in truth *(John 4:24)*. When you enter prayer with a thankful heart, your requests are no longer demands—they become conversations. Your heart becomes less entitled and more surrendered.

Every time you pray, you should be thankful. Please don't ever pray, make your requests, and then walk away without showing how grateful you are to God. *Psalm 100:4* reminds us to *"Enter into His gates with thanksgiving, and into His courts with praise: be thankful unto Him, and bless His name."* That means we begin our time with The Father by recognizing His goodness before we ever bring a request.

If you do something for someone and they don't say thank you, I'm sure you would think that person is ungrateful. Well, if that's how we feel about each other, how much more should we be mindful of showing gratitude to God, who gave us everything—including the breath we use to say, "Thank You"?

The Prayer of Worship

Genesis 4:25-26 (AMP)

"25 Adam knew [Eve as] his wife again; and she gave birth to a son, and named him Seth, for [she said], 'God has granted another child for me in place of Abel, because Cain killed him.' 26 To Seth, also, a son was born, whom he named Enosh (mortal man, mankind). At that [same] time men began to call on the name of The Lord [in worship through prayer, praise, and thanksgiving]."

The prayer of worship acknowledges God for who He is. We can see in Genesis 4:25-26 for the first time that mankind began to call on the name of The Lord. I love how this scripture sums it all up by saying that worship is expressed through prayer, praise, and thanksgiving.

When we worship, we recognize God as God. He is Savior, Lord, King, and Master. When we open our mouths to pray, worship should be one of the first things uttered. While we worship, we transcend into praise, declaring specifically what He has done while thanking Him.

This type of prayer doesn't have to be structured in a prayer setting. It is not only meant for inside the church. It's not only meant for times when you kneel to pray. The prayer of worship can be done in many ways. For instance, while cleaning the house, a person may listen to Christian music and begin to worship, praise, and be thankful to The Lord. Another may go into worship while driving in their car, having a moment with The Father. And yes, even while gardening, singing accolades to Him, a person can worship. The prayer of worship is not restricted to a time and place, so be free to worship.

The Prayer of Consecration

Matthew 26:39 (AMP)

"And after going a little farther, He fell face down and prayed, saying, 'My Father, if it is possible [that is, consistent with Your will], let this cup pass from Me; yet not as I will, but as You will.'"

The prayer of consecration sets oneself apart to follow God's will. Consecration is to be set apart for a higher purpose. Jesus knew He would go through the hardest thing He could imagine in over thirty years of life, and He needed His Father's strength for the task. There are things that God is calling you to, and just because you are called to it doesn't mean that it will be easy. You may be called to the pastorate and become overwhelmed with the responsibility. The prayer of consecration in this instance would not only mean you are saying yes to the call, but you are showing God that you depend on Him for it. You essentially say, "I can't do this alone. I rely on You for everything." You may want a way out, but it is the course that God has set for you, and Jesus, at the end of it, said, "not my will but thou will."

God wants a yes from you. It may be that addiction that you need to give up, and you may see it as a hard thing. But not your will, but His will be done in you. It may be an unhealthy emotional relationship, and you can't get away, but in the prayer of consecration, you let go of them and let God's will be done. The prayer of consecration comes down to a convergence with the course of your destiny and purpose, and the death of your will for His will to be done in your life.

The Prayer of Intercession

1 Timothy 2:1 (AMP)

"First of all, then, I urge that petitions (specific requests), prayers, intercessions (prayers for others), and thanksgivings be offered on behalf of all people."

In this prayer, it's about the needs of others. You put aside your desires and fervently go to God on behalf of someone else. You stand in proxy for that individual and represent them before The Father.

In charismatic and Pentecostal circles, intercessory prayer may be an intense, dynamic time with music and fervent prayer. However, in your own personal prayer time, when you get to the basics of intercession, make sure to pray as earnestly for another as you would for yourself. You stand in as a proxy for that individual and their needs. Whether that person can pray for themselves or not, if you decide to intercede for the person, then do it with all of your heart, even if God asks you to pray for someone who doesn't like you. God may call you to intercede for the one who gets on your last nerve, and God expects you to pray with all you have.

Practical Applications

To cultivate a rich and varied prayer life, here are some practical applications you can use:

1. Incorporate Different Types of Prayer: Dedicate time to practice each type of prayer in your routine, whether daily, weekly, or as led by The Spirit.

2. Keep a Prayer Journal: Document prayers, reflections, and how God responds, which can build faith and guide your growth.

3. Seek Accountability: Join prayer groups or partners who encourage consistency and help navigate challenges in your spiritual walk.

4. Integrate The Word of God: Scripture is essential to prayer, anchoring your requests, thanksgiving, and declarations in biblical truth.

The diversity of prayer types reflects the dynamic nature of your relationship with God. By engaging in these prayers, you nurture your connection with The Father, grow spiritually, and fulfill your role as His representative on earth.

Type of Prayer	Key Purpose	Supporting Scripture
Prayer of Faith	Trusting God for specific results	James 5:15
Prayer of Agreement	Uniting with others in faith for one request	Matthew 18:19
Prayer of Request	Bringing personal needs before God	Philippians 4:6
Prayer of Thanksgiving	Expressing gratitude to God	1 Thessalonians 5:18
Prayer of Worship	Honoring God for who He is	Psalm 95:6, John 4:24
Prayer of Consecration	Submitting your will to God's will	Luke 22:42
Prayer of Intercession	Praying on behalf of others	1 Timothy 2:1, Ezekiel 22:30

Chapter Reflection and Activation

1. Which type of prayer do you use most often, and which one do you tend to neglect or feel less confident in practicing?

2. Think about a recent prayer you prayed—was it a prayer of faith, agreement, request, thanksgiving, worship, consecration, or intercession? What led you to pray that way?

3. How does understanding the different types of prayer help you grow in spiritual maturity and deepen your relationship with God?

4. What adjustments can you make to begin incorporating more variety and intentionality into your daily or weekly prayer life?

Now that you've learned the different types of prayer—faith, agreement, request, thanksgiving, worship, consecration, and intercession—you're starting to see how dynamic and layered prayer truly is. But knowing the types is just the beginning.

In the next chapter, we'll talk about the one thing every type of prayer must have in order to be effective: faith. Without it, even the most passionate prayer falls short. Let's build on what you've learned by going deeper.

CHAPTER 3:
THE PREREQUISITE TO PRAYER

Now that I have discussed a few facets of prayer, it is necessary to address the prerequisite to prayer. You likely know what a prerequisite is. It is something required before something else—it sets the stage for what comes next. For example, the soil must be prepared and watered in gardening before seeds are planted. A house must have a solid foundation before erecting the walls, and the roof is set in place. Before baking a cake, the ingredients must be gathered and measured. We often handle many prerequisites in daily activities, even without being aware of them. In college, specific courses require that you complete others first. These are examples of prerequisites. Similarly, in the spiritual realm, prayer has a prerequisite. Unfortunately, it's often overlooked. That prerequisite is faith.

What Is Faith?

Faith[1] is defined as "confidence or trust in a person or thing; belief that is not based on proof."

---

[1] "Dictionary.com | Meanings and Definitions of English Words." *Dictionary.com*, 23 June 2025, www.dictionary.com/browse/faith.

Hebrews 11:1 (AMP)

"Now faith is the assurance (title deed, confirmation) of things hoped for (divinely guaranteed), and the evidence of things not seen [the conviction of their reality—faith comprehends as fact what cannot be experienced by the physical senses]."

Notice it begins with "Now faith..." not past faith, not future faith—but present, active, current faith. "Now faith" means right-now trust. If you have the title deed to a property, you own it. Likewise, when you possess faith, you take ownership of what you believe God for. The moment you receive that "deed" of faith in your heart, God guarantees what you hope for. Even if you can't see it in the natural, you can know it's yours in The Spirit.

Without Faith, It's Impossible

Hebrews 11:6 (AMP)

"But without faith it is impossible to [walk with God and] please Him, for whoever comes [near] to God must [necessarily] believe that God exists and that He rewards those who [earnestly and diligently] seek Him."

So, how can you expect to please God if you don't first believe that He exists? We should not just believe in His existence but also believe that He is a rewarder, a good Father who honors the sincere pursuit of Him. Some people pray "just in case"

God exists. But faith is not a gamble—it's conviction. Real prayer begins with the confidence that He is and that He responds.

Consistency: A Faith Essential

Another vital aspect of faith is consistency. You can't believe today, doubt tomorrow, and then expect what you prayed for.

Matthew 7:7 (AMP)

> *"Ask and keep on asking, and it will be given to you; seek and keep on seeking, and you will find; knock and keep on knocking, and the door will be opened to you."*

Faith is persistent. Faith does not give up when the door doesn't open the first time. You must have an intentional, enduring mindset. Faith is not just what you believe; it's how long you're willing to believe without seeing the result.

Believe You've Received

Mark 11:24 (AMP)

> *"For this reason I am telling you, whatever things you ask for in prayer [in accordance with God's will], believe [with confident trust] that you have received them, and they will be given to you."*

This principle of prayer must be understood: you believe before you receive. God responds to your faith, not just your words.

Faith and Doubt Cannot Coexist

Hebrews 10:35 (AMP)

"Do not, therefore, fling away your [fearless] confidence, for it has a glorious and great reward."

Faith must be protected. Don't allow disappointment, delay, or fear to rob you of your confidence. Doubt and faith cannot live in the same space. Where one dominates, the other dies. It is like oil and water—they don't mix. Faith must be nurtured, guarded, and reinforced constantly.

How To Build Up Your Faith

You might say, "There are times when I lack faith." Let's explore how to strengthen your faith using *Mark 9:17-27*.

In that passage, a father brought his mute son to Jesus, desperate for deliverance. After describing the torment his son had faced since childhood, the father pleaded, *"If You can do anything, have compassion on us and help us."* Jesus responded, *"If you can believe, all things are possible to him who believes."* The man cried out, *"Lord, I believe; help my unbelief!"*

That statement is both honest and intuitive. He believed—but he was also struggling. And Jesus didn't reject him; He delivered the boy.

The verses of *Mark 9:17-27* give us practical steps for building faith:

1. *Acknowledge areas of doubt.* Ask God sincerely to help your unbelief.

2. *Be transparent in prayer.* Speak openly about what you're struggling to believe.

3. *Fight for your faith.* Rebuke doubt and unbelief daily in prayer. Faith is a spiritual battleground.

4. *Guard your ears.* Avoid voices that instill fear, doubt, or discouragement, especially when seeking to believe in God for something significant.

5. *Immerse yourself in Scripture.* Study scriptures where faith prevailed and God responded.

6. *Meditate on truth.* Speak verses over your life until they become part of your mindset. For example, *Proverbs 3:5a* says, *"Trust in The Lord with all thine heart."* Declare that until it takes root.

7. *Be patient while you wait.* Some prayers take years. God's timing is not ours, but His promises are sure.

Great People of Faith

To fully understand the power and impact of faith in action, we must examine the examples found in Hebrews 11:4–40. This chapter is often called the "Hall of Faith" because it highlights individuals who overcame trials, obeyed God's call, and performed great acts—all by faith.

Let's look at a few of them and draw the key themes relevant to our lives and prayer journey:

- Abel offered a better sacrifice than Cain, not because of the gift itself, but because of the faith behind the offering. His faith still speaks, even after death.

- Enoch walked with God so closely that he didn't even see death—he was taken up because his faith pleased God.

- Noah, though warned of events not yet seen, built an ark. That action, rooted in faith, saved his entire household. Faith acts even when logic fails.

- Abraham obeyed God's call to go to an unknown land. He lived like a foreigner, trusting God's unseen promises. He even offered up Isaac, believing God could raise him from the dead if necessary. His wife, Sarah, conceived a child long past childbearing years—all because they trusted God's Word.

- Isaac, Jacob, and Joseph blessed their descendants and prophesied about their future by faith, even on their deathbeds.

- Moses, born into privilege in Egypt, chose hardship over comfort, aligning with God's people. He forsook the treasures of Egypt, kept the Passover, led Israel out of Egypt, and crossed the Red Sea—all by faith.

- Rahab, though once a prostitute, was saved because she believed in the God of Israel and welcomed the spies in peace.

- Then Paul, the author of Hebrews, rapidly lists others: Gideon, Barak, Samson, Jephthah, David, Samuel, and the prophets—people who conquered kingdoms, upheld justice, escaped flames, shut lions' mouths, and endured intense persecution.

Some even faced death, were stoned, and imprisoned—not because they lacked faith, but because they clung to it. The world wasn't worthy of them. They wandered in deserts and caves, driven by an unshakeable belief in God's promises.

Yet, verse 39 tells us:

"All of these, though they gained divine approval through their faith, did not receive the fulfillment of what was promised, because God had us in mind."

They believed—even when they didn't receive. That's the kind of enduring, resolute, heaven-focused faith we must pursue. It's faith that connects us to God, no matter the result. The common thread among all these people? They acted by faith. Not by impulse, not by emotion, not by fear—but by trusting in God. They built, moved, sacrificed, prayed, obeyed, and endured—all because they believed. And their belief wasn't in outcomes alone—it was in the character of God. So what about you?

Can you hold on when the outcome is unclear? Will you still pray when the answer is delayed? Will you remain confident in God even when things don't make sense? Can you trust Him as your foundation, your fortress, your Father?

Faith is the prerequisite to prayer because prayer communicates with The One you cannot see but must believe. Without faith, prayer becomes a ritual. With faith, prayer becomes powerful.

May your faith be stirred, your doubts be silenced, and your prayers rise boldly before the throne of grace—because the God who heard Abel, Enoch, Noah, Abraham, Sarah, Moses, and countless others is listening for you.

Chapter Reflection and Activation

1. When you pray, do you genuinely believe God hears and will respond, or do you sometimes pray "just in case"? What does that reveal about your faith?

2. How has doubt shown up in your prayer life, and what steps can you take to guard or strengthen your faith going forward?

3. Which example from the "Hall of Faith" (Hebrews 11) spoke to you the most, and why? How can you apply that example to your current season?

4. What scriptures or practices can you begin using to reinforce your faith before and after you pray?

Faith is what gives prayer its power. Without it, prayer becomes routine—just words. But with it, prayer becomes a force that moves mountains and brings heaven to earth. Now that you understand the role of faith in your prayer life, it's time to learn how Jesus Himself taught us to pray. In the next chapter, we'll walk through the Model Prayer—not just to recite it, but to live it.

CHAPTER 4:
THE MODEL PRAYER

You likely have read, heard, and memorized The Model Prayer *(Matthew 6:5-15)*. However, have you ever considered the definition of the word model and how this word relates to The Model Prayer? The word model[2] is defined as *"a standard or example for imitation or comparison."*

Through The Model Prayer, Jesus showed us an example of how to pray, and He expects us to imitate it based on the structure, not the exact words used. This statement is not to suggest that we not memorize and recite The Model Prayer, but remember it is a model, an example that we are to imitate as well.

Matthew 6:5-15 (AMP)

"5 Also, when you pray, do not be like the hypocrites; for they love to pray [publicly] standing in the synagogues and on the corners of the streets so that they may be seen by men. I assure you and most solemnly say to you, they [already] have their reward in full. 6 But when you pray, go into your most

---

[2] "Dictionary.com | Meanings and Definitions of English Words." *Dictionary.com*, 24 June 2025, www.dictionary.com/browse/model.

private room, close the door, and pray to your Father who is in secret, and your Father who sees [what is done] in secret will reward you. [7] And when you pray, do not use meaningless repetition [don't babble] as the Gentiles do, for they think they will be heard because of their many words. [8] So do not be like them [praying as they do]; for your Father knows what you need before you ask Him. [9] Pray, then, in this way: 'Our Father, who is in heaven, Hallowed be Your name. [10] Your kingdom come, Your will be done on earth as it is in heaven. [11] Give us this day our daily bread. [12] And forgive us our debts, as we have forgiven our debtors [letting go of both the wrong and the resentment]. [13] Do not lead us into temptation, but deliver us from evil. [For Yours is the kingdom and the power and the glory forever. Amen.] [14] For if you forgive men their trespasses, your heavenly Father will also forgive you. [15] But if you forgive not men their trespasses, neither will your Father forgive your trespasses."

Matthew Chapter 6 is part of a long sermon or extensive teaching by Jesus, beginning in chapter 5, and is commonly referred to as The Sermon on the Mount.

Matthew 5:1-2 (AMP)

"[1] When Jesus saw the crowds, He went up on the mountain; and when He was seated, His disciples came to Him. [2] Then He began to teach them, saying"

Jesus addressed many powerful subjects in His Sermon on the Mount, but in the specific set of verses of Chapter 6, verses 5-15, He focused on prayer. Though the model prayer is found in verses 9-13, the related teachings in verses 5-8 and 14-15 are equally significant and could not be excluded.

Personal Prayer Time

Jesus spoke about personal prayer time with The Father. Jesus took time out of this long sermon to talk about prayer, which shows how important prayer is and why we should never take it lightly.

E.M. Bounds says in the book *Answered Prayer*[3]:

> *"Prayer has been the special distinction of all God's saints. It has been the secret of their power. The energy and the soul of their work have come from their prayer lives. Because the need for help outside of man is so great – given man's natural inability to always judge kindly, justly, and truly and to act on the Golden Rule – prayer is enjoined by Christ to enable man to act in all these things according to the divine will. By prayer, the ability is secured to feel the law of love, to speak according to the law of love, and to do everything in harmony with the law of love."*

---

[3] Bounds, E. M. *Answered Prayer*. Whitaker House. 1994. Page 7.

This quote impacted me deeply. The fact that prayer is described as the special distinction of God's saints reveals its importance. It distinguishes us as a people of prayer but also implies something about those who refuse to pray. Those who refuse to pray, still expect the best from God. But let me ask you this question. If you don't take time to pray, how can you have true access to the power of God without it?

I grew up in a time when many of the saints of old declared the statement "more prayer, more power, little prayer, little power." This term has long been used to encourage believers everywhere to pray. How can we become fortified to do anything for The Lord without the secret power of prayer?

The most effective people in The Kingdom of God, whose ministries are impactful, often cite prayer as a key to their success. Prayer is where the energy and soul of their work originate. Hence, some men and women of God are identified by phrases like, "That is a praying Man of God" or "My mother was a praying mother." These phrases highlight the significance of prayer and its transformative power. Men and women built their lives as living testimonies and examples of having a prayer life. We should do the same.

Hypocrites/Showoffs/Sincere Prayer

Verse 5 starts with a key phrase: *"When you pray."* It doesn't say "if you pray" or *"maybe* if you decide to pray." Jesus said, "When." Prayer is not optional—it is a necessity. We should consider Jesus' words as a command: Pray. Jesus said it. That settles it.

If you ever hear a teaching that says Christians no longer need to pray, know that it is heresy. Turn to them and say, *"But Jesus said 'When you pray.'"* Jesus didn't give us an option.

Jesus also warns against praying like hypocrites, who love to pray publicly to be seen by people. He didn't critique their act of praying but their intentions. They sought the accolades of people rather than cultivating a sincere relationship with The Father.

Vine's Dictionary explains that the term "hypocrite[4]" originates from Greek and Roman theater, referring to stage actors who wore masks to amplify their voices. Metaphorically, it came to mean "a dissembler" or someone who pretends to have virtues or beliefs they do not possess. Hypocrites put on a façade and present their lives in a godly manner. This behavior is not pleasing to The Lord.

So when you pray, don't perform—connect. Don't seek to impress—seek to be heard by The Father. Prayer is not about volume, vocabulary, or visibility; it's about the heart. God is not moved by how eloquent we sound, but by how honest we

---

[4] Vine, W. E., and Merrill Unger. *Vine's Complete Expository Dictionary of Old and New Testament Words: With Topical Index*. Thomas Nelson, 1996. Page 316

are. Let your prayer life be real, private, and powerful. The Lord sees what's done in secret—and that's where the true reward lies.

The Prayer Room

In verse 6, Jesus again says, *"When you pray."* He then instructs us to go into a private room, away from distractions. The focus is on sincerity rather than seeking public recognition. God sees the heart, and those who secretly pray to Him will be rewarded openly.

In verse 6, Jesus is not referring to corporate prayer, which I discussed in Chapter 2. He is speaking about one-on-one time with The Father. When you do that, and if you desire to pray to God and for God to speak back to you, then be in the right environment so you can spend time with Him.

I think of it this way: if you are in a relationship, there are times you want to get away from all the distractions of the world because nothing else matters other than being in the presence of the one you love. As it is with them, so it should be with God (and much more with God). Nothing else matters than being in the presence of God, whom we love. Spending time with Him without distractions is so important.

Praying vs. Babbling

Verse 7 highlights the issue of meaningless repetition. Jesus says, *"When you pray, do not use meaningless repetition as the Gentiles do, for they think they will be heard because of their many words."*

Praying for extended periods is not an issue, but prayer should be heartfelt and meaningful, not incoherent or repetitive, to appear pious. The word babble[5] " is defined as *"to utter sounds or words imperfectly, indistinctly, or without meaning."*

When you pray, you pray with specific meaning, not based on the length of the prayer. You want to go to God with your requests, not babbling and nonsense. For example, if you want something from someone, and you say, "Buy me a red dress in my size." That description is vague because it does not specify the design, cut, length, or designer. It doesn't give them any details. But if you say, "I want this red dress I saw in this magazine shown here in a size 7," you're giving specific aspects, including a picture for them to see. It's essential that when you pray, be specific with God.

A specific request to The Lord with clarity about what you desire will be more effective than praying for three hours without clarity. Now, being specific in prayer doesn't mean we will receive what we request, for what we request may not be

---

[5] "Dictionary.com | Meanings and Definitions of English Words." *Dictionary.com*, 29 May 2025, www.dictionary.com/browse/babble.

in His will. However, when we're specific, we don't give heed to babbling or repetitions, which Jesus speaks against.

So Then, Why Pray?

Verse 8 may seem confusing: *"For your Father knows what you need before you ask Him."* Some might question why prayer is necessary if God already knows our needs. The key lies in Jesus' repeated instruction: *"When you pray."*

Even though God knows our needs, He desires to hear our voice. He wants us to articulate our needs, demonstrating our dependence on Him. *Philippians 4:6 (AMP)* reminds us: *"Do not be anxious or worried about anything, but in everything [every circumstance and situation] by prayer and petition with thanksgiving, continue to make your [specific] requests known to God."*

In This Manner

In verse 9, Jesus said, *"Pray, then, in this way: 'Our Father, who is in heaven, Hallowed be Your name."* We must acknowledge who God is before we do anything else in prayer. Address Him. Don't skip over acknowledging Him and start asking for things—that is just plain rude. Don't skip over worship because you want to get what you need off your chest.

Before we make requests to God, we must first honor Him. Imagine walking into a courtroom and immediately shouting your demands to the judge before the session even begins. You would likely be held in contempt. There is an order—an approach—that honors the authority of the room. Likewise, when we enter into prayer, we must remember we are addressing The King of Kings. Start with worship. Start with reverence. Let God know that you recognize who He is before you ask for what you need.

You may not be as articulate in prayer as you have heard others, but start reading Psalm. The writings of the psalmists present God in many ways, giving Him so many accolades. Use the Psalms to help you build your knowledge of who God is. Then, use who you know Him to be to worship Him. Speak to Him about who He is to you.

Yield to Him

In verse 10, Jesus says, *"Your kingdom come, Your will be done, On earth as it is in heaven."* After acknowledging Him, we are to yield to Him, His kingdom, His desires. We come before Him humbly. We submit to His authority. We bow before Him in His majesty. We accept His sovereignty. We want His will to be done.

If we come to Him wanting His will to be done, we have already conditioned ourselves at the beginning of prayer and ultimately for our lives. We condition ourselves to always allow His will to be done. Thus, when He lets us know that what we want is not His will, we submit to Him instead of coming out of prayer to do what we wish to: doing something to edify our flesh but detrimental to our soul.

Now Make Your Request Known

In verse 11, we see the first time a request is made. Jesus said, *"Give us this day our daily bread."* After the other two parts of prayer, you can now ask God to provide for you. This request is not only about food. You should want a daily provision of God's favor, protection, joy, and peace. Every day, you should wish to have money in your pockets and not be in need. God expects you to ask for these things—the new job you seek, the promotion that seems out of reach, or the new home your family needs.

Humanity will always want something. Many want the latest vehicle, the newest phone, or the biggest television. But what is it that you need? In this part of the prayer, dealing with your requests, you are also encouraged to pray for others. Don't think this time is only for your specific requests—engage in intercessory prayer for others. (Learn more about intercessory prayer later in Chapter 5.)

Forgiveness

In verse 12, we see that we must be introspective. Jesus said, *"And forgive us our debts, as we have forgiven our debtors [letting go of both the wrong and the resentment]."* Sometimes, I will pray this part before my requests. As I write this now, I wonder why Jesus placed this part of the prayer after the request.

After you worship and acknowledge The Father, He is open to hearing your requests. The more you speak to The Father and spend time with Him, the more you become aware of where you have fallen short of His Word. We recognize that we may ask God for things, but there is an expectation to live for Him and do His will.

Ask God to forgive you for all the things you have done—sins of omission and commission. Be specific as well. You know when you've messed up: the time you lied, didn't show love, or told someone off without acting in the character of God. There's no need to be unclear in your personal prayer time with The Father.

(Notice I said personal prayer time because sometimes people leading corporate prayer make it very personal—that's not the time or place.)

God forgives us, but we must also forgive. Be transparent with The Father about your hurt caused by others. Ask Him to help you let go of resentment. Linger in prayer if you need to. God is a healer of your emotions if you allow Him to be.

One last thing about forgiveness: I'm sure you don't want your prayers to go unanswered because of unforgiveness. Sometimes, that bitterness or resentment isn't just toward people—but toward God. Now, let's be clear—God doesn't need our forgiveness because He never does wrong. Everything He allows or withholds is filtered through His wisdom and love. But let's be honest—there are moments when we feel disappointed, let down, or even angry with The Lord because things didn't go the way we hoped. Don't bury that. Bring it into your prayer time. Be real with The Father about the pain you've felt. He can handle your honesty, and He can heal your heart. Let go of the offense—not because God did something wrong, but because holding onto it can cloud your trust and stall your prayers. Release it. Let Him restore your peace.

Deliverance

As we come to the last verse in The Model Prayer, we ask God, as Jesus said, *"Lead us not into temptation, but deliver us from evil."* The verse sounds like God might place us in the path of temptation. Yet, the New Living Translation of verse 13 reads, *"And don't let us yield to temptation, but rescue us from the evil one,"* which further clarifies the previous interpretation.

God is not leading us into temptation, which is further backed by *James 1:13 (AMP)* which says, *"Let no one say when he is tempted, 'I am being tempted by God' [for temptation does not originate from God, but from our own flaws]; for God cannot be tempted by [what is] evil, and He Himself tempts no one."*

God is never leading us into temptation, but rather the intent of Matthew 6:13 is this: Before we give in to temptation, ask God to rescue us, which we should do daily, because temptations may arise to draw us away from the things of God.

End with Worship

Jesus ends The Model Prayer with, *"For Yours is the kingdom and the power and the glory forever. Amen."* How you end your prayer should mirror how you start it, with worship. Don't rush through to "Amen." Bask in His presence, allowing God to speak if He has more to say.

As previously stated, prayer is two-way communication, so take time to listen. Sometimes, the thing you've asked God for begins to take shape while you are still in prayer.

In my own experiences, God moved on me during prayer, granting me peace and strength. These intimate times with The Father are priceless, and I cherish them. As you pray, you too will experience God moving upon you.

Forgiveness Repeated

In the following two verses, verses 14 and 15, Jesus speaks about forgiveness again. These verses are not a part of The Model Prayer, but requires that we study them as they are related to prayer.

God knows the hurts and pain others have caused you, but as a child of God, there is a different mindset you should have about people who do you wrong. There is no tit-for-tat in The Kingdom of God.

If you resist forgiving others, then God will not forgive you. This action calls for real soul-searching in prayer. Sometimes, I have asked God, "If there is anything that I am holding in my subconscious, let me know." Similar to this statement of mine in prayer, you must allow God to reveal to you if you're dealing with unforgiveness. If there's something that occurred with a person that you don't want to talk about, you might be dealing with unforgiveness. Sometimes unforgiveness can be you shutting a person out of your mind, thinking that makes it easier for you to cope because they're not around. However, how do you feel if a name comes up in conversation? If you happen to see them, what are your thoughts? Do feelings of resentment or hatred rise? Would you want harm to befall them? Forgive them quickly and then pray.

God doesn't want you to pray and remain the same. If you are praying as you should, there should be a change in you, whether people see it or not.

Paul says in *Ephesians 4:31-32 (AMP)*

> *"31 Let all bitterness and wrath and anger and clamor [perpetual animosity, resentment, strife, fault-finding] and slander be put away from you, along with every kind of*

malice [all spitefulness, verbal abuse, malevolence]. ³² Be
kind and helpful to one another, tender-hearted
[compassionate, understanding], forgiving one another
[readily and freely], just as God in Christ also forgave you."

Paul didn't say let *some* go; he said let *all* go. You shouldn't release some things and hold on to others. He said to forgive one another readily and freely. In other words, someone shouldn't have to force you to forgive. You shouldn't hold a grudge against someone until you receive an apology.

Do you realize it never says, "Only forgive when you get an apology?" You may ask someone for an apology, and they may feel they didn't do anything wrong. Will you choose not to forgive in that case? There are even people who, after receiving an apology, still refuse to forgive. Based on Luke 17:4, we have no excuse not to forgive.

Luke 17:4 (The Message)

"Even if it's personal against you and repeated seven times through the day, and seven times he says, 'I'm sorry, I won't do it again,' forgive him."

Matthew 18:21-22 (AMP)

"²¹ Then Peter came to Him and asked, 'Lord, how many times will my brother sin against me, and I forgive him and let it go? Up to seven times?' ²² Jesus answered him, 'I say to you, not up to seven times, but seventy times seven.'"

Jesus wasn't suggesting you keep a tally and stop forgiving at 491 offenses. Instead, He made a clear distinction: forgiveness must be absolute and total. It may feel unfamiliar or even unnatural, but that is what The Bible requires.

"The ultimate proof of total forgiveness takes place when we petition The Father to let those who have hurt us off the hook—even if they have hurt not only us, but also those close to us."[6]

Praying To Another?

John 14:6 (AMP)

"Jesus said to him, 'I am the [only] Way [to God] and the [real] Truth and the [real] Life; no one comes to The Father but through Me.'"

1 Timothy 2:5 (AMP)

"For there is [only] one God, and [only] one Mediator between God and mankind, the Man Christ Jesus."

These verses highlight an essential point: nowhere in The Model Prayer does it say we should pray to another person. Jesus is the only way to The Father and the only Mediator between God and mankind.

---

[6] Kendall, R. T. *Total Forgiveness: When Everything in You Wants to Hold a Grudge, Point a Finger, and Remember the Pain - God Wants You to Lay it All Aside*. Charisma House, 2010.

Sometimes people have honest questions about prayer, such as: *Should I direct prayer to anyone other than God? Should I seek another spiritual mediator in my prayer life?* Scripture makes it clear that prayer is directed to God, through Jesus Christ. We do not need another go-between.

The Bible does not instruct believers in Christ to pray to anyone other than God. And when Scripture speaks about attempting to consult the dead or seek spiritual contact outside of God, it is presented in the context of forbidden practices—sorcery, witchcraft, necromancy, and divination—activities strongly condemned in scripture:

Leviticus 20:27 (AMP)

"A man or woman who is a medium [who pretends to consult the dead] or who is a spiritist shall most certainly be put to death and be stoned with stones; their blood is on them."

Deuteronomy 18:10-13 (AMP)

"[10] There shall not be found among you anyone who makes his son or daughter pass through the fire [as a sacrifice], one who uses divination and fortune-telling, one who practices witchcraft, or one who interprets omens, or a sorcerer, [11] or one who casts a charm or spell, or a medium, or a spiritist, or a necromancer [who seeks the dead]. [12] For everyone who does these things is utterly repulsive to The Lord; and because of these detestable practices The Lord your God is

*driving them out before you. [13] You shall be blameless
(complete, perfect) before The Lord your God."*

In the one instance where someone sought a word from the deceased prophet Samuel (1 Samuel 28:7-19), it was not presented as a model for prayer or spiritual guidance. It was a clear warning about crossing spiritual boundaries that God never authorized.

So, the question becomes simple: Who do we pray to? We pray to God. Only God can hear our prayers. Only God can answer our prayers. And the only way we come to The Father is through Jesus Christ.

No one else can mediate with God for us (1 Timothy 2:5). If Jesus is the only Mediator, then we should not treat anyone else as a mediator in prayer.

Romans 8:26-27 (AMP) describes The Holy Spirit interceding for us as well:

*"[26] In the same way the Spirit [comes to us and] helps us in
our weakness. We do not know what prayer to offer or how to
offer it as we should, but the Spirit Himself [knows our need
and at the right time] intercedes on our behalf with
sighs and groanings too deep for words. [27] And He who
searches the hearts knows what the mind of the Spirit is,
because the Spirit intercedes [before God] on behalf of
God's people in accordance with God's will."*

With Jesus Christ and The Holy Spirit already interceding for us before The Father, Scripture does not indicate that we should seek intercession from anyone who has passed away. Only God hears prayer. Only Jesus mediates prayer. Only The Holy Spirit intercedes according to the will of God.

Pray The Will of God

God does not answer prayers based on who is praying. God answers prayers based on whether they are asked according to His will. *1 John 5:14-15 (AMP)* says:

"14 This is the [remarkable degree of] confidence which we [as believers are entitled to] have before Him: that if we ask anything according to His will, [that is, consistent with His plan and purpose] He hears us. 15 And if we know [for a fact, as indeed we do] that He hears and listens to us in whatever we ask, we [also] know [with settled and absolute knowledge] that we have [granted to us] the requests which we have asked from Him."

So how do you know if you're praying God's will? Start with His Word. When your prayers line up with Scripture, you can pray with boldness, knowing God hears and will respond. It's not about fancy words or spiritual status—it's about alignment. When your heart lines up with God's heart, your requests gain Heaven's attention. So don't just pray what you want—pray what He wants from you. That's where the power is.

Chapter Reflection and Activation

1. How does viewing The Lord's Prayer as a *model* rather than a script change the way you approach prayer?

2. Which part of The Model Prayer—worship, surrender, request, forgiveness, or deliverance—do you find most challenging, and why?

3. In what ways has repetition, performance, or tradition shaped your prayer life? What changes do you feel God is calling you to make?

4. How does understanding forgiveness as a condition for answered prayer affect the way you pray—and the way you relate to others?

The Lord's Prayer isn't just a recitation—it's a roadmap. It shows us how to approach God with worship, humility, and trust.

In the next chapter, we'll take what you've learned and apply it outward. It's time to shift from personal prayer to praying on behalf of others—what the Bible calls intercession.

CHAPTER 5:
INTERCESSORY PRAYER

Common words you will hear in many charismatic Pentecostal churches worldwide are intercession or intercessory prayer. But what is it? What does it mean to intercede on behalf of a person, your family at large, your church, your city, your government, or the world?

My scripture of emphasis will be *1 Timothy 2:1 (KJV),* which says:

"I exhort therefore, that, first of all, supplications, prayers, intercessions, and giving of thanks, be made for all men."

How do we distinguish supplications from prayer, intercession, and giving thanks? There must be a reason why Paul spoke of the four. Let's break this verse down.

- Supplication[7] is the action of asking or begging for something earnestly or humbly. To apply this definition directly to our walk with God, supplication relates to our posture in prayer. It's about coming boldly and humbly before the throne of God, having

---

[7] "Dictionary.com | Meanings and Definitions of English Words." *Dictionary.com,* 11 Apr. 2025, www.dictionary.com/browse/supplication.

met the prerequisite of faith. It's about asking, not demanding. We are making our requests known to God, not telling God what He should do for us.

- Prayer - As previously stated, prayer is two-way communication with God, seeking a relationship with Him and a deeper level of intimacy.
- Giving of Thanks - To give thanks to God is to praise Him not only for what He is doing in your life but also for what He has done and is getting ready to do for you.

What Is Intercession?

Now, let me take a step into intercession. Intercession[8] is to plead on behalf of another, serving as a go-between, mediation, intervening, and interposing on someone's behalf, and standing in prayer in the gap for someone else.

To simplify these terms all associated with prayer, I often think of each in this easy manner:

- Supplications – humble request for help from God.

- Prayer – a two-way conversation with God.

- Intercession – standing in the gap for others before God.

---

[8] "Dictionary.com | Meanings and Definitions of English Words." *Dictionary.com*, 28 Feb. 2024, www.dictionary.com/browse/intercession.

- Giving Thanks – gratitude for what God has done and will do.

In intercession, praying for your individual needs is not intercession. Praying for yourself is not intercession, while praying for one's family is. Intercessory prayer is not a request for personal things. It is a selfless prayer. When you intercede, you stand in proxy for someone or something.

Intercession is intentional. You don't slip into intercession. Intercession is on purpose. It is often preceded by a burning desire for someone or something that causes one to enter intercession.

Getting caught up with your desires, aspirations, and the things you want God to do for you that haven't come to pass yet is easy. You may worship and praise God, be overwhelmed with the presence of The Lord, and not once pray for anyone else. We, as believers, are not called to be selfish and let everything be all about ourselves. Thus, sometimes, when The Spirit of God impresses upon us a person or situation, intercession is a means of praying for that person or situation.

How To Pray in Intercession?

When you decide to enter into intercession for another, you should pray as hard as you would for yourself. The same level of intensity and vigor that you pray with when asking God for something you deeply desire should be the same level—or even greater—when you go before The Lord on behalf of another. Not only with intensity but with specificity.

Let's put some scripture to this point. *Job 16:21 (AMP)* says:

"Oh, that a man would mediate and plead with God [for me] just as a man [mediates and pleads] with his neighbor and friend."

To mediate and plead with God means to focus on what you are interceding for and make it so much a part of you that you feel it is happening to you. With that feeling, now plead with God with your very being.

We must realize that intercession is not a passive prayer. You should not be nonchalant when entering intercessory prayer. You can't be lackadaisical in intercessory prayer. A "whatever will be, will be" kind of mindset does not belong here. Unless God specifically tells you not to pray about a thing, then actively pray.

James 5:16b (AMP)

"...The heartfelt and persistent prayer of a righteous man (believer) can accomplish much [when put into action and made effective by God—it is dynamic and can have tremendous power]."

You may think, *"Well, I am not an Elder or Pastor or hold some high position in the church. I am just a brother or a sister. I am not on any auxiliary.*" Or if you are on one, you may say, *"I am just an usher and consider myself insignificant compared to others I see operating in different positions in the pulpit.*" The Bible didn't say only those with big or prominent titles can intercede. The Scripture of James 5:16b makes it so clear. The prayer of a righteous believer can accomplish much when put into action.

I want you to meditate on those words. When the enemy has you feeling like, *"Who are you to pray?"* When you feel like you are not hearing an answer. When you feel like God is not moving quickly enough on what you prayed for, remember that you need to keep praying because you can accomplish much. But wait—there are conditions James speaks of:

1. **It should be heartfelt.**

   What a key to intercession. Don't do it just because someone may be asking you. Do it from the heart.

2. **It should be persistent.**

   In other words, don't pray once; if God doesn't move for the person or change the situation, don't decide to quit. The Word of The Lord speaks to you about being persistent.

In the book *The Essential Guide to Prayer*[9], *by Dutch Sheets*, the author writes:

"A lack of endurance is one of the greatest causes of defeat, especially in prayer. We don't wait well. We're into microwaving; God, on the other hand, is usually into marinating."

3. Put it into action.

Don't just contemplate what you're going to do. Don't simply think about it. Please don't read this and do nothing. Learn what you should do, and put it into action.

Who Should Intercession Be Made For?

Who should intercession be made for? The simple answer: all men, all women, all boys, and all girls.

- You might think, "But what if I can't stand that person?" God may still call you to intercede for them.

- "But what if they hate me?" Yes, God may say to pray for them.

- "What if they stabbed me in the back (figuratively)?" Even then, God may call you to pray for them.

---

[9] Sheets, Dutch. *The Essential Guide to Prayer: How to Pray with Power and Effectiveness*. Bethany House, 2017.

He is calling you to pray, as previously stated, as fervently as you would for yourself.

Let's explore some scriptures that bring further clarity to emphasize this point.

Matthew 5:43-44 (AMP)

"43 You have heard that it was said, 'You shall love your neighbor (fellow man) and hate your enemy.' 44 But I say to you, love [that is, unselfishly seek the best or higher good for] your enemies and pray for those who persecute you."

The Word of The Lord will always challenge us to do what would not be the norm. The Word is clear: desire the absolute best for others, even your enemies.

- You might say, "You don't understand what they said about me." Desire the best for them.

- You might say, "You don't know how they treated me." Desire the best for them.

Notice that The Word didn't say to try to befriend your enemies. It didn't say to go out to eat with your enemies. It says to desire the best for them and pray for them, yes, even your enemies, who persecute you. Is it a hard thing? Yes, it can be, but God doesn't only require the easy things from us.

We should also pray for people in government and those in authority.

1 Timothy 2:2 (AMP) says to pray for:

"Kings and all who are in [positions of] high authority, so that we may live a peaceful and quiet life in all godliness and dignity."

You might ask, "So, if I'm a Democrat, should I only pray for those in my party? Or if I'm a Republican, should I only pray for those in office who share my views?" That's not what The Word says. God doesn't deal with political parties or those in power based on our preferences. You should pray for "all" who are in positions of authority, even if you didn't vote for them.

And please—do not pray for their harm. We must be people of God who hold to The Word of God, not our preferences, letting our emotions direct our actions. We aim to live peaceful and quiet lives in all godliness and dignity. Instead of praying for their demise, pray that they make wise decisions for our city, state, country, and even the world.

Can I suggest something? There is so much chaos in the land because not enough people are standing in the gap. There aren't enough believers interceding. Many people are so divided by politics that the bigger picture is overlooked. Prayer should be at the forefront of politics and in every aspect of life. It doesn't matter if a Christian loves those in authority or dislikes others in authority.

God will intervene. So, stop complaining about the person you didn't vote for or the person you did vote for who isn't fulfilling their promises.

Pray regarding all levels of authority: mayors, governors, the president, senators, representatives, school board members, police chiefs, and so on. Intercede for your neighborhood. Is the place you live in starting to become unrecognizable? Pray. Get others to pray with you until you see a change in your community.

Jeremiah 29:7 (AMP)

"Seek peace and well-being for the city where I have sent you into exile and pray to The Lord on its behalf; for in its peace (well-being) you will have peace."

It's so clear: if—and only if—you pray for where you live, you will have peace there. You want peace on the job? Pray. You want peace in your church? Pray. You want peace in your family? Pray. You want peace in the schools? Pray. pray, pray, pray!

Purpose of Intercessors and Intercession

What is the purpose of intercession and intercessors? Intercessors are needed in The Kingdom of God. You may ask, "Doesn't God know all? Doesn't He see it all? Why did this happen? Why did that happen on His watch?" You may not realize that God is calling individuals on the earth who will pray His will and His heart concerning matters. God works through His intercessors to effect change on the planet. The world around you is influenced by prayer. God works with His intercessors, not independently of them. God will not intervene unless there are people who will pray.

All believers are Christ's representatives on the earth. We are His Ambassadors.

> "Notice that nowhere in The Bible does God instruct us to ask for things that are going to happen automatically. He never tells us to ask for the sun to shine, for air to breathe, or for gravity to perform its work. He only tells us to ask for things He has made contingent on us. He is so determined to work through our prayers, He has said it is possible to 'have not because we ask not...' (*James 4:2 KJV*).[10]"

Read 2 Chronicles 7:14 (AMP) to understand the purpose of intercessors and intercession further:

"And My people, who are called by My Name, humble themselves, and pray and seek (crave, require as a necessity) My face and turn from their wicked ways, then I will hear

---

[10] Sheets, Dutch. *The Essential Guide to Prayer: How to Pray with Power and Effectiveness.* Bethany House, 2017.

[them] from heaven, and forgive their sin and heal their land."

There is a condition that God has placed in The Word of The Lord that still stands today: if the people of God would humble themselves, pray, and seek the face of God, things would change. Let's unpack that. The Word says to pray, as if doing something methodically, and seek—crave after God. Turn from doing evil, and then God will fulfill His part of the promise.

You are needed on the earth. If you don't meet the conditions – to humble and turn, to pray and seek His face - how can you expect God to fulfill His part?

There is healing for the land. It's in the mouths of the intercessors. It's in the mouths of the believers. It's in the mouths of you and me. Too often, we have kept our mouths shut, and instead of healing, we have bleeding. If we would rise in the earth and be the intercessors that God has called us to be—not just churchgoers, not just people who pray only about our own needs, but people who seek God on behalf of others—imagine what this world could look like.

God's Promise to Us

John 14:14 (AMP)

"If you ask Me anything in My Name [as My representative], I will do it."

Did The Bible use the word '*anything*' related to asking Him to do something? Do you realize now the weight you hold as an intercessor once you have met God's conditions? Ask anything in His Name, and He will do it. Nothing is too hard. Nothing is too impossible for God to do. If God has promised something, He must hold to His Word concerning it. His Name gives us access to the throne room. But don't just call on His Name without being willing to do your part.

John 15:16 (AMP)

"You have not chosen Me, but I have chosen you and I have appointed and placed and purposefully planted you, so that you would go and bear fruit and keep on bearing, and that your fruit will remain and be lasting, so that whatever you ask of The Father in My Name [as My representative] He may give to you."

This scripture makes it even clearer. We must do our part and bear fruit. He chose us and intentionally placed us in our respective states and countries.

So, ask yourself: What type of fruit are you bearing? How are you living? Are your prayers being rejected because of rotten fruit? He wants you and me to bear fruit continually.

What fruit is being spoken of? *Galatians 5:22-23 (AMP)* says:

"[22] But the fruit of The Spirit [the result of His presence within us] is love [unselfish concern for others], joy, [inner]

peace, patience [not the ability to wait, but how we act while waiting], kindness, goodness, faithfulness, [23] gentleness, self-control. Against such things there is no law."

God requires us to display these characteristics in our daily lives. As we represent Him on the earth by displaying these characteristics, we should represent Him as intercessors on the job, in our homes, communities, and beyond. Then, when we ask in His name, we shall have what we request (John 14:14). We shall have those things that are in His will and plan.

Chapter Reflection and Activation

1. Who in your life has God placed on your heart to consistently pray for, and how might interceding for them impact both of you?

2. When was the last time you prayed for someone with the same intensity and specificity you use when praying for yourself?

3. What misconceptions have you had about intercessory prayer, and how did this chapter bring clarity?

4. How can you become more intentional and disciplined in practicing intercessory prayer, especially when it's for people you may not naturally feel drawn to?

Intercession may seem simple, but it carries weight. When you pray for others, you're stepping into a deeper level of spiritual responsibility—and love. There's power in that kind of prayer, and in the next chapter, we'll take a closer look at just how far that power can reach.

CHAPTER 6:
THE POWER AND PURPOSE OF INTERCESSION

As I stated, intercession is not just an act of prayer; it's a calling, a responsibility, and a privilege entrusted to God's people. In a world filled with challenges, chaos, and spiritual battles, the role of the intercessor stands as a vital pillar in The Kingdom of God.

In this chapter, we will explore the profound impact of intercessory prayer. From the biblical examples of Abraham, Isaac, and Moses, we'll see how God moves powerfully through those willing to pray. You'll discover that intercession is not limited to pastors or church leaders—it is a role every believer can step into. As you read, I encourage you to reflect on the power of prayer, the purpose of standing in the gap, and the blessings that come to those who commit to this sacred calling.

Are you ready to take your place as an intercessor and partner with God to bring His will to earth? This chapter will show you how.

Proactive, Not Reactive

For many believers, prayer is treated like a fire extinguisher—something you reach for only when something is burning. But what if prayer could stop the fire from breaking out in the first place? As intercessors, we are not just called to respond after the damage is done—we are called to watch, guard, and cover before the enemy even makes his move.

Being proactive in prayer means you stay ahead of what's coming. It means you pray even when everything seems fine, because you understand the assignment of the enemy is often subtle and delayed. When things are peaceful, when your home is calm, when your job is stable—that's the time to build a wall of spiritual protection around it all.

You may say, "I live in a great neighborhood. There's no violence here. It's quiet. It's safe." Trust me—live long enough, and things can change. Demographics shift. Values shift. What once felt like paradise can suddenly become problematic. That's not fear speaking; that's discernment. Don't wait until the peace is gone to seek The Lord—pray while it's still present.

Being a proactive intercessor doesn't require a title. You don't need to be a Pastor, Elder, or Evangelist. You don't need a microphone. All you need is the burden and the willingness to obey God's prompting. You, my brother, can stand in the gap. You, my sister, can be the watchman on the wall for your block, your city, your church, your family.

There are times when God has placed someone on my heart—people I've never met, sometimes even celebrities—and told me to pray. He didn't give me any explanation or show me the connection of what to pray. He only gave me a burden. And in those moments, I've learned to respond immediately. You never know whose life may be hanging in the balance because God was searching for someone to intercede.

So, pray for your neighborhood. Pray for your child's school. Pray for churches you don't attend. Pray for regions you've never visited. You don't need all the details—just obey. There are spiritual battles being fought that you can't see with your natural eyes. But your prayers can make all the difference. Don't just be a believer who reacts. Be a believer who watches. Be one who prepares. Be one who prays.

Intercessory Prayer in Action

Ezekiel 22:30 (AMP)

"I searched for a man among them who would build up the wall and stand in the gap before Me for [the sake of] the land, that I would not destroy it, but I found no one [not even one]."

What a powerful scripture! In this verse, God sought an intercessor to stand in the gap. It makes me wonder: how many times in this day has God searched for an intercessor who could have prevented some of the calamities we've heard about, only to find none? How many things could have been averted—accidents, disasters, painful moments—had someone been willing to pray? How many times have we, as people, been too busy with other things and decided not to pray?

Years ago, I watched a documentary about a man named John Ramirez, who was once a Satan worshipper[11]. He was involved in astral projection[12], which is defined as *"a supernatural phenomenon in which a person's astral body is said to separate from the physical body and travel to or in a different plane of existence."*

He employed this practice to create chaos in various neighborhoods within the realm of the spirit.

Two things he shared about intercession stood out as incredibly powerful:

1. He mentioned that as he attempted to astral project into a specific neighborhood, he couldn't do anything because he saw three women praying on a street corner. Their names were never mentioned, but their

---

[11] The 700 Club. "Out of the Devil's Cauldron." *YouTube*, 27 June 2012, www.youtube.com/watch?v=tAoGlU7Uy-w.

[12] "Dictionary.com | Meanings and Definitions of English Words." *Dictionary.com*, www.dictionary.com/browse/Astral%20Projection.

commitment to praying for their community prevented the enemy from gaining a foothold in that area.

2. On another occasion, he attempted to enter someone's house, but he was unable to do so because of a bright light surrounding the house. That home had been covered in prayer.

This testimony from a former Satan worshipper underscores the profound impact of prayer. The prayers of the righteous thwart the plans of the enemy. We must not take the power of prayer lightly.

Can You Be Trusted to Be God's Intercessor?

What does it mean to be trusted as God's intercessor? When you are called to intercession, you must not take it lightly. There is a certain level of confidentiality that comes with the role.

There may be times when someone, recognizing the anointing on your life, comes to you and asks for prayer about a deeply personal matter. The only thing you are meant to do with that information is to pray. Likewise, God may reveal things about a person that require your intercession—things so sensitive that if others knew, it might embarrass the individual.

As an intercessor, you must guard what has been entrusted to you, which is not an opportunity for gossip. You should not share this information with a friend, spouse, or anyone else.

God has not authorized you to do that. Instead, He expects you to take that burden to Him in prayer.

Moreover, you should not go to the person to verify what God has revealed. If you have a relationship with God and know He has spoken to you about someone, why would you need to validate it with them? Your job is clear: just pray. Pray exactly what God tells you to pray, and continue praying until He releases you from the assignment. Do not go beyond what God has instructed you to do.

When God Says, "Do Not Pray"

What if God tells you not to pray about a specific matter? Can you obey His voice when He asks you to refrain from interceding? That might sound shocking at first, especially to those of us who have learned that prayer is always the correct answer. But as a discerning intercessor, sensitivity to the voice of God is essential.

Let's look at what happened in *Jeremiah 7:16 (AMP)*:

"Therefore, do not pray for this people [of Judah] or lift up a cry or entreaty for them or make intercession to Me, for I do not hear you."

In this example, God had already made His judgment. The people ignored warnings, rejected His Word, and persisted in rebellion. Prayer wasn't going to change it—the sentence was already passed. God wasn't being cruel; He was being just.

Sometimes, God's silence or restriction on prayer is a sign that His will is already set in motion.

That doesn't mean we walk away from our post as intercessors. It means we listen even more carefully, because every command from God isn't about doing something— sometimes it's about ceasing, waiting, or redirecting. That's maturity. Sometimes God will test our spiritual growth by instructing us to stop praying about a matter, not because He's distant, but because He wants to know: Can you trust Me even when I close a door?

Let's not confuse God's voice with the enemy's just because the instruction is unfamiliar. The enemy will attempt to sow confusion or instill condemnation. But God's instruction— even if it challenges you—will always align with His Word and His Spirit.

Isaiah 55:8–9 reminds us:

"8 'For My thoughts are not your thoughts, neither are your ways My ways,' saith the Lord. 9 'For as the heavens are higher than the earth, so are My ways higher than your ways, and My thoughts than your thoughts.'"

Sometimes, God is not asking you to pray—He's asking you to trust. There are times when God will assign you to intercede and times when He will release you from that assignment. He may redirect your prayers to others, or call you to be still and watch Him move.

Let me be clear: The statement "Do Not Pray" is not about refusing to pray in general—this is about a specific divine instruction. The key is discernment. And discernment comes through time spent with Him.

So if God ever says, "Don't pray for this," don't panic. Don't doubt His love. Just remember—He's still in control. He's still good. He's still God. And even in silence, He's speaking.

The Blessing for the Intercessor

The next thing I want to address is the blessings for the intercessor. I intentionally placed this section here because we often become more focused on what God will do for us than on the actual assignment and call we are meant to fulfill in our lives.

Job 42:8-10 (AMP)

"8 Now therefore, take for yourselves seven bulls and seven rams, and go to My servant Job, and offer up a burnt offering for yourselves, and My servant Job will pray for you. For I will accept him [and his prayer] so that I may not deal with you according to your folly, because you have not spoken of Me the thing that is right, as My servant Job has. 9 So Eliphaz the Temanite and Bildad the Shuhite and Zophar the Naamathite went and did as The Lord told them; and The

Lord accepted Job's prayer. [10] The Lord restored the fortunes of Job when he prayed for his friends, and The Lord gave Job twice as much as he had before."

I love these verses because they demonstrate intercession in several ways. First, it highlights God's need for an intercessor on the earth. Second, it shows how God trusted Job to intercede on behalf of his friends. Finally, it reveals the blessings Job received as a result of his obedience in intercession. Job's restoration did not occur until he selflessly prayed for others. This statement teaches us that if we are committed to being intercessors, God will not forget our needs. He hears the prayers you've offered for yourself, sees what you've endured, and yet calls you to pray for others—even in the midst of your trials.

What's the mark of spiritual maturity? When life is at its worst, the inclination is often to pray only for personal needs. Yet, God might say, "I've heard you; now pray for this person." Obedience in intercession brings blessings to those who answer God's call.

Intercessors in The Word

The Bible showcases many examples of intercessors who stood in the gap on behalf of others. Let's look at Abraham, Isaac, and Moses.

Abraham:

" ¹⁶ Then the men got up from there, and looked toward Sodom; and Abraham walked with them to send them on the way. ¹⁷ The LORD said, "Shall I keep secret from Abraham [My friend and servant] what I am going to do, ¹⁸ since Abraham is destined to become a great and mighty nation, and all the nations of the earth will be blessed through him? ¹⁹ For I have known (chosen, acknowledged) him [as My own], so that he may teach and command his children and [the sons of] his household after him to keep the way of The Lord by doing what is righteous and just, so that The Lord may bring upon Abraham what He has promised him." ²⁰ And The Lord said, "The outcry [of the sin] of Sodom and Gomorrah is indeed great, and their sin is exceedingly grave. ²¹ I will go down now, and see whether they have acted [as vilely and wickedly] as the outcry which has come to Me [indicates]; and if not, I will know." ²² Now the [two] men (angelic beings) turned away from there and went toward Sodom, but Abraham remained standing before The Lord. ²³ Abraham approached [The Lord] and said, "Will You really sweep away the righteous (those who do right) with the wicked (those who do evil)? ²⁴ Suppose there are fifty righteous [people] within the city; will You really sweep it away and not spare it for the sake of the fifty righteous who are in it? ²⁵ Far be it from You to do such a thing—to strike the righteous with the wicked, so that the

righteous and the wicked are treated alike. Far be it from You! Shall not the Judge of all the earth do right [by executing just and righteous judgment]?" 26 So The Lord said, "If I find within the city of Sodom fifty righteous [people], then I will spare the entire place for their sake." 27 Abraham answered, "Now behold, I who am but dust [in origin] and ashes have decided to speak to The Lord. 28 If five of the fifty righteous are lacking, will You destroy the entire city for lack of five?" And He said, "If I find [at least] forty-five [righteous people] there, I will not destroy it." 29 Abraham spoke to Him yet again and said, "Suppose [only] forty are found there." And He said, "I will not do it for the sake of the forty [who are righteous]." 30 Then Abraham said [to Him], "Oh, may The Lord not be angry, and I will speak; suppose thirty [righteous people] are found there?" And He said, "I will not do it if I find thirty there." 31 And he said, "Now behold, I have decided to speak to The Lord [again]. Suppose [only] twenty [righteous people] are found there?" And The Lord said, "I will not destroy it for the sake of the twenty." 32 Then Abraham said, "Oh may The Lord not be angry [with me], and I will speak only this once; suppose ten [righteous people] are found there?" And He said, "I will not destroy it for the sake of the ten." 33 As soon as He had finished speaking with Abraham The Lord departed, and Abraham returned to his own place."

Because of this great intercessor, Abraham, God was willing to spare the cities of Sodom and Gomorrah if only ten righteous people could be found. Abraham reasoned with God, demonstrating the power and weight of intercession. He stood in the gap for people he may not have even known.

This passage challenges us to consider our role as intercessors. Do we use our influence with God to intercede for our neighborhoods, cities, and nations? Intercession has the power to avert judgment and bring mercy. Abraham's example reminds us that even one faithful intercessor can make a profound difference.

Imagine having many Abrahams in this generation—intercessors committed to standing in the gap. What might the world look like? Could it be that some calamities occur because of a lack of intercessors? Abraham's story demonstrates that one person's prayers can avert judgment. Now, imagine the impact of many righteous people rising to intercede for the land.

Isaac:

Genesis 25:21-24 (AMP)

> *"[21] Isaac prayed to The Lord for his wife, because she was unable to conceive children; and The Lord granted his prayer and Rebekah his wife conceived [twins]. [22] But the children struggled together within her [kicking and shoving*

one another]; and she said, 'If it is so [that The Lord has heard our prayer], why then am I this way?' So, she went to inquire of The Lord [praying for an answer]. [23] *The Lord said to her, '[The founders of] two nations are in your womb; And the separation of two nations has begun in your body; The one people shall be stronger than the other; And the older shall serve the younger.'* [24] *When her days to be delivered were fulfilled, behold, there were twins in her womb."*

Many people desperately try to have children but cannot. In biblical times, they didn't have access to the fertility treatments and medical interventions we have today. What they had was prayer. Here we see Isaac interceding for his wife, Rebekah, because she was barren. The result? Not just one child, but twins. This passage highlights the power of intercession to bring forth life from that which was barren.

In today's advanced world of medicine and technology, we often turn to these resources first, leaving prayer as our last option. While it is a blessing to have these advancements, it is crucial to remember that our ultimate reliance should be on God.

Isaac's intercession reminds us that prayer should never be an afterthought—it is powerful enough to create life where there was none.

Moses:

Deuteronomy 9:9 (AMP)

*"When I went up the mountain to receive the tablets of stone,
the tablets of the covenant which The Lord made with you, I
remained on the mountain forty days and forty nights; I did
not eat food or drink water."*

Deuteronomy 9:12-14 (AMP)

*"12 Then The Lord said to me, 'Arise, go down from here
quickly, for your people whom you brought from Egypt have
acted corruptly. They have quickly turned aside from the way
which I commanded them; they have made (cast) a molten
image for themselves.' 13 Furthermore, The Lord said to me,
'I have seen this people, and indeed, they are stiff-necked
(stubborn, obstinate) people. 14 Let Me alone, so that I may
destroy them and wipe out their name from under heaven;
and I will make of you a nation mightier and greater than
they.'"*

Deuteronomy 9:18-20 (AMP)

*"18 Then, as before, I fell down before The Lord for [another]
forty days and forty nights; I did not eat food or drink water,
because of all the sin you had committed by doing what was
evil in the sight of The Lord to provoke Him to anger. 19 For I
was afraid of the anger and absolute fury which The Lord
held against you, [enough divine fury] to destroy you, but*

The Lord listened to me that time also. [20] The Lord was very angry with Aaron, angry [enough] to destroy him, so I also prayed for Aaron at the same time."

Wow—if Moses wasn't the definition of an intercessor, I don't know who is. In this text, Moses went up the mountain to receive the tablets of the commandments and fasted for 40 days and 40 nights. During this time, the Israelites turned to idolatry, angering God so much that He was ready to eradicate them and raise a new nation from Moses' lineage.

But Moses didn't accept this plan. Instead, he interceded for the people, fasting for another 40 days and 40 nights to plead with God on their behalf. Moses' persistence and tenacity in prayer saved the Israelites, demonstrating his deep commitment to his calling as an intercessor.

What a powerful example of perseverance in prayer! Moses did not give up until he saw results. Imagine what could happen if we approached intercession with the same level of dedication and commitment.

Chapter Reflection and Activation

1. What stood out to you about the power and results of intercession in the biblical examples shared in this chapter?

2. Have you ever felt a persistent spiritual urge to pray for someone or something? What did you learn through that experience?

3. How does understanding the *purpose* of intercession—beyond just outcomes—reshape the way you view your role in prayer?

4. In what areas (family, church, city, nation) do you feel called to intercede more boldly, and how will you begin answering that call?

You've seen how intercession isn't just emotional—it's impactful. It invites God's intervention and releases His will in the lives of others. But to stand in that role with confidence, you need to understand your spiritual authority. In the next chapter, we'll explore what it means to pray with boldness, to speak with heaven's backing, and to walk in the authority God has already given you.

CHAPTER 7:
PRAYING WITH AUTHORITY

There is a common saying called "P.U.S.H." in Pentecostal circles, which stands for "Pray Until Something Happens." This phrase emphasizes persistence in prayer. At the same time, it is essential to focus on what we are praying about and what we may be praying against. In the realm of the spirit, we have God who is for us and opposing forces—Satan and his kingdom—against us.

Bind It and Loose It

The phrase *"binding and loosing"* might sound like lofty religious language, but it's actually one of the most powerful tools we've been given as believers. It speaks to spiritual authority—authority that Jesus entrusted to those who follow Him and walk in agreement with His Word.

In *Matthew 18:18 (AMP)*, Jesus said:

"I assure you and most solemnly say to you, whatever you bind [forbid, declare to be improper and unlawful] on earth shall have [already] been bound in heaven, and whatever you loose [permit, declare lawful] on earth shall have [already] been loosed in heaven."

This wasn't just a phrase for church discipline—it was a declaration of heaven's partnership with faithful believers. To bind something means to shut it down in the spirit. To loose something means to release it in the earth. In prayer, we don't fight aimlessly—we speak with heaven's authority.

We bind every plan, spirit, thought, or influence that does not line up with God's will. We bind confusion, division, addiction, fear, anxiety, lust, and everything the enemy tries to release in our homes, churches, communities, or minds. And when we bind it, we do it in Jesus' name, knowing it aligns with the righteousness of heaven.

After binding, we loose what is godly. We loose peace, healing, clarity, financial provision, restored families, and every good thing God has already made available. We loose breakthrough. We loose victory. We loose deliverance. As Jesus said in *John 14:13, "And whatsoever ye shall ask in My name, that will I do, that The Father may be glorified in The Son."*

Binding and loosing is not spiritual fantasy—it's spiritual responsibility. But we must do it with reverence, prayer, and alignment with The Word of God. The power to bind and loose doesn't work just because we said the right words. It works when we walk in faith, live in obedience, and pray according to His will.

It's not just about spiritual warfare either. Binding and loosing also applies to relationships, mindsets, opportunities, and even how we handle the enemy's attacks. When something shows up in your life that God didn't send, you have the authority to bind it. When you've been waiting on something God has promised, you have the authority to loose it into the atmosphere through prayer and declaration.

Let's be clear—this isn't about controlling people or circumstances, but about exercising agreement with Heaven. God has given you the keys. The question is: will you use them?

Operating with Kingdom Authority

Let's take a moment to define "authority" for clarity. Authority is: "the power to determine, adjudicate, or otherwise settle issues or disputes; jurisdiction; the right to control, command, or determine; a power or right delegated or given."[13]

As I begin to discuss Kingdom authority, I want to emphasize that operating in Kingdom authority is not about holding lofty titles or engaging in religious performance. It's about understanding your God-given position as a believer. Authority in The Kingdom is not earned through status; it is given through relationship and revelation. When you truly

---

[13] "Dictionary.com | Meanings and Definitions of English Words." *Dictionary.com*, 24 June 2025, www.dictionary.com/browse/authority.

know who Jesus is and walk in obedience to His Word, you gain access to His delegated power on the earth.

In *Matthew 16:18b–19a* (KJV), Jesus told Peter:

"...Upon this rock I will build My church; and the gates of hell shall not prevail against it. And I will give unto thee the keys of the kingdom of heaven..."

This wasn't about physical keys. It was spiritual authority. Jesus was saying, "Because you know who I am, you can now operate on My behalf." That same authority is available to every believer who has received the revelation of Christ—not just with their minds, but in their hearts.

To operate with Kingdom authority means that we no longer speak from fear, doubt, or defeat. We speak from our seat in heavenly places.

Ephesians 2:6 (KJV)

"And hath raised us up together, and made us sit together in heavenly places in Christ Jesus."

This verse is more than symbolic—it is a spiritual reality. When you know your seat, you speak from that seat.

Kingdom authority empowers us to address situations in our lives that are out of alignment with God's will. You can declare peace where there is chaos, healing where there is sickness, and restoration where there is brokenness. These declarations aren't spiritual hype—it's biblical truth. *Luke 10:19* reminds us, *"Behold, I give unto you power… over all the power of the enemy: and nothing shall by any means hurt you."*

Let me be clear—authority doesn't mean arrogance. It's not about shouting louder or sounding more spiritual. Authority is exercised in alignment with The Word of God and the leading of The Holy Spirit. It's spiritual maturity that says, "I only say what My Father says. I only loose what heaven approves."

Dr. Cindy Trimm talks about Kingdom authority. She said,

> *"The time has come when God has stirred up the hearts of all believers to rise and take their rightful places as His official representatives in the earthly realm. Our role is to activate and enforce the authority God has given us. As an empowered believer, you should no longer be satisfied with standing on the sidelines or accepting anything from the enemy. There is a real battle going on. There are no demilitarized zones in this battle. Thank God we have been assured that, in this warfare, we are fighting the good fight of faith. The outcome has been decided, and our victory*

has been incorporated into the equation. It is time to beat the devil at his own game. "[14]

So, how do you walk in Kingdom authority? First, stay rooted in The Word. Second, remain sensitive to The Holy Spirit. Third, speak only what heaven authorizes. Don't bind what God hasn't bound. Don't loose what heaven has not approved. This is not about manipulation—it's about alignment.

Finally, remember that authority is not for show—it's for service. We are called to use this authority to set captives free, intercede for others, build up the Church, and advance the mission of Christ. You don't need a microphone to walk in authority. You need revelation, obedience, and boldness. You have authority—now walk in it.

Warring in The Spirit with Your Armor On

You may be part of a church and have heard the term spiritual warfare. Let me begin by discussing spiritual warfare, or 'warring in the spirit,' through prayer.

Ephesians 6:11-17 (AMP) says:

"[11] Put on the full armor of God [for His precepts are like the splendid armor of a heavily armed soldier], so that you may be able to [successfully] stand up against all the

---

[14] Trimm, Cindy. *The Rules of Engagement: The Art of Strategic Prayer and Spiritual Warfare.* Creation House, 2005.

schemes and the strategies and the deceits of the devil. [12] For our struggle is not against flesh and blood [contending only with physical opponents], but against the rulers, against the powers, against the world forces of this [present] darkness, against the spiritual forces of wickedness in the heavenly (supernatural) places". [13] Therefore, put on the complete armor of God, so that you will be able to [successfully] resist and stand your ground in the evil day [of danger], and having done everything [that the crisis demands], to stand firm [in your place, fully prepared, immovable, victorious]. [14] So stand firm and hold your ground, having tightened the wide band of truth (personal integrity, moral courage) around your waist and having put on the breastplate of righteousness (an upright heart), [15] and having strapped on your feet the gospel of peace in preparation [to face the enemy with firm-footed stability and the readiness produced by the good news]. [16] Above all, lift up the [protective] shield of faith with which you can extinguish all the flaming arrows of the evil one. [17] And take the helmet of salvation, and the sword of the Spirit, which is The Word of God".

Let's break this down. First, we are told to put on the full armor of God. The AMP version explains that God's *precepts* are like the splendid armor of a heavily armed soldier. A *precept* is defined as: *"a commandment or direction given as a rule of action or conduct; an injunction as to moral conduct."*[15]

Before you speak with authority or come against what the enemy is doing, you must first deal with who *you* are. Are you fortified in God's Word? Are you aligned with His precepts? If so, you're in a position to wage spiritual war.

Verse 12 makes something very clear: our struggle is not against flesh and blood. It's not about arguing with people or fighting visible battles—it's about recognizing the unseen spiritual forces operating behind the scenes. Paul uses war language here for a reason. Just like earthly wars involve strategy, ideologies, and authority structures, spiritual warfare also involves ranks and real enemies.

Just as God has a divine order of authority—archangels like Michael (who leads the warring angels) and Gabriel (who delivers messages)—the kingdom of darkness also has its hierarchy. Some demons hold more authority than others. This knowledge isn't meant to frighten you, but to inform and equip you. You must recognize what you're up against so you can fight *correctly*.

---

[15] "Dictionary.com | Meanings and Definitions of English Words." "---." *Dictionary.com*, 13 June 2025, www.dictionary.com/browse/precept.

You don't fight a spiritual battle with emotional outbursts or fleshly reactions. You fight it in The Spirit—with the armor of God.

Notice that verse 11 says "full armor" and verse 13 says "complete armor." Paul is stressing total preparedness. It's not enough to have partial protection; you need the *whole* armor to withstand the evil day. Without it, you will live in defeat rather than victory.

Let's look at each piece:

1. *The Belt of Truth (Ephesians 6:14)*
   Paul tells us to "tighten the wide band of truth around your waist," which refers to *integrity*—walking honestly and upright before God and man. Integrity is defined as: *"adherence to moral and ethical principles; honesty; the state of being whole, entire, or undiminished."*[16]
   To be whole in yourself means to be consistent in character. As believers, we must not just appear godly—we must *be* godly. Paul warned Timothy of those who would have a form of godliness but deny its power.

---

[16] "Dictionary.com | Meanings and Definitions of English Words." *Dictionary.com*, 24 June 2025, www.dictionary.com/browse/integrity.

2 Timothy 3:2–5 (AMP) says:

"² For people will be lovers of self [narcissistic, self-focused], lovers of money [impelled by greed], boastful, arrogant, revilers, disobedient to parents, ungrateful, unholy and profane, ³ [and they will be] unloving [devoid of natural human affection, calloused and inhumane], irreconcilable, malicious gossips, devoid of self-control [intemperate, immoral], brutal, haters of good, ⁴ traitors, reckless, conceited, lovers of [sensual] pleasure rather than lovers of God, ⁵ holding to a form of [outward] godliness (religion), although they have denied its power [for their conduct nullifies their claim of faith]. Avoid such people and keep far away from them."

This warning is still relevant today. We must examine ourselves to ensure our conduct doesn't contradict our faith or nullify the authority God wants us to walk in.

2. *The Breastplate of Righteousness (Ephesians 6:14)*
   This piece of armor protects your *heart*. The breastplate of righteousness guards the core of who you are—your emotions, motives, and moral center.

Proverbs 4:23 (AMP)

"Watch over your heart with all diligence, for from it flow the springs of life."

When you allow unrighteousness into your heart—
whether it's bitterness, offense, jealousy, or
unconfessed sin—you open yourself to spiritual attack.
But when your heart is covered in righteousness, your
decisions align with God's will, not your emotions.

3. *The Shoes of the Gospel of Peace (Ephesians 6:15)*
   Paul says to have your feet "strapped with The Gospel
   of Peace," which speaks of stability and readiness.
   When you know God's Word and walk in His peace,
   you don't run when the enemy attacks—your footing
   is secure in God. You remain firmly rooted in your
   identity and mission.

4. *The Shield of Faith (Ephesians 6:16)*
   "Above all, lift up the shield of faith." Why? Because
   faith shields you from the fiery arrows of the enemy—
   doubts, lies, discouragement, fear, shame, and guilt.
   The enemy will whisper things like:
   - "God forgot about you."
   - "You're not good enough."
   - "You'll never be healed."
   - "God won't come through."
   But faith extinguishes every lie. When you raise your
   shield, you refuse to believe the enemy's narrative.
   You hold fast to God's truth.

5. *The Helmet of Salvation (Ephesians 6:17)*
    The mind is the battlefield. The helmet protects your thoughts. Like the character *Juggernaut* in Marvel movies—whose helmet shielded him from telepathic attacks—your spiritual helmet guards you from mental attacks of doubt, confusion, and deception. The enemy targets your mind because if he can corrupt your thinking, he can influence your decisions, emotions, and faith. Guard your mind with the assurance of your salvation and identity in Christ.

6. *The Sword of The Spirit (Ephesians 6:17)*
    The sword is your only offensive weapon—and it is *The Word of God.* When Jesus was tempted in the wilderness, He didn't argue with Satan. He responded with: *"It is written."*
    A Word-filled response cuts through the enemy's lies. But you must *know* the Word in order to use it. Your sword must be sharp and ready.

Lessons From the Wilderness

In Matthew 4:1–11 (AMP), we see Jesus being led into the wilderness to be tempted by the devil. This spiritual battle was one of identity, trust, and authority. And Jesus didn't fight back with emotions—He responded with The *Word*.

Matthew 4:3–4

*"³ And the tempter came and said to Him, 'If You are the Son
of God, command that these stones become bread.' ⁴ But
Jesus replied, 'It is written and forever remains written, Man
shall not live by bread alone, but by every word that comes
out of the mouth of God.'"*

Then in verses 5–6, the enemy tried again—this time using
scripture out of context:

*"⁵ Then the devil took Him into the holy city [Jerusalem] and
placed Him on the pinnacle (highest point) of the
temple. ⁶ And he said [mockingly] to Him, "If You are the
Son of God, throw Yourself down; for it is written, 'He will
command His angels concerning You [to serve, care for,
protect and watch over You]'; and 'They will lift you up
on their hands, So that You will not strike Your foot against a
stone.'"*

Jesus again responded in verse 7:

*"On the other hand, it is written and forever remains written,
'You shall not test The Lord your God.'"*

Finally, the devil tried to tempt Jesus with power and glory:

Verses 8–10

*"⁸ Again, the devil took Him up on a very high mountain and
showed Him all the kingdoms of the world and the glory*

[splendor, magnificence, and excellence] of them; [9] *and he said to Him, "All these things I will give You, if You fall down and worship me."* [10] *Then Jesus said to him, "Go away, Satan! For it is written and forever remains written, 'You shall worship The Lord your God, and serve Him only.'"*

After the third time, verse 11 says:

"Then the devil left Him; and behold, angels came and ministered to Him [bringing Him food and serving Him]."

Let this encourage you: when you endure spiritual battle in obedience and with The Word, God sends help. Heaven will minister to you after you've stood your ground.

But don't miss the principle behind Jesus' victory. It wasn't just about quoting scripture. *James 4:7 (AMP)* teaches us the same pattern:

"So submit to [the authority of] God. Resist the devil [stand firm against him] and he will flee from you."

Many people try to resist the devil without *first submitting* to God. But authority flows from submission. You must follow God's order: submit, then resist—and the devil will flee.

When you enter prayer, understand that you are engaging in a war. The enemy is relentless, and you must be equally relentless in your authority. Be prepared. Be rooted. Be unmoved. Refuse to fight in the flesh. Instead, war in The Spirit.

When life overwhelms you and you're tempted to fight back, complain, argue, or spiral out of control, take a pause. Refocus. Declare, "I'm giving this to God."

Many of the saints of old would say, "I'm going to turn it over to The Lord." And they meant it. They had confidence that prayer changed things. They rebuked the devil. They called him a liar. They saw him coming a mile away.

We must return to that mindset. We must become believers who pray with authority—unapologetically.

Know who you are. Know what you carry. Stand firm. You are a warrior. You are victorious. You are authorized.

Chapter Reflection and Activation

1. When you pray, do you approach God as a child with access or as a stranger hoping to be heard? What has shaped that mindset?

2. What does it mean to you to pray "with authority," and how does this differ from casual or timid prayer?

3. Which scriptures or truths from this chapter reminded you of your identity and authority in Christ? How can you begin to pray from that position?

4. Are there any areas of your life where you've been praying *about* the problem instead of *speaking to* the problem in faith? What shift can you make starting now?

____

Learning to pray with authority isn't about having all the right words—it's about knowing who you are and trusting who God is. That confidence changes everything.

CLOSING STATEMENT

As you have come to the end of this book, I pray that this has given you further insights into prayer like never before. I hope that this will encourage you to pray without ceasing.

Hopefully, you gathered from this book that prayer is not an option and that it has many facets. I am glad this book is another step in further developing your prayer life.

Thank you for reading this book, and please keep it as a resource and share it with others who would like to know more about prayer.

ABOUT THE AUTHOR

Dr. Paul M. Bromfield is a devoted minister, teacher, and theologian with a passion for breaking down The Word of God in a way that is both accessible and transformational. With over two decades of ministry experience, Dr. Bromfield has faithfully served in various capacities within the local church—from teaching to preaching The Gospel on multiple platforms. Known for his practical, no-nonsense teaching style, he is especially gifted in equipping believers with foundational truths that build a strong, unshakable faith.

Dr. Bromfield holds a Doctorate in Theology, a journey of study and spiritual formation that deepened his understanding of biblical principles and gave rise to this book and its accompanying series, *Let's Get Back to Basics.* This volume, explicitly focused on the subject of prayer, emerges not only from theological training but from lived experience—a life marked by consecration, consistent intercession, and a desire to restore the body of Christ to its essential spiritual disciplines.

In addition to his academic and ministerial work, Dr. Bromfield serves as a mentor and counselor to many, often guiding individuals who feel spiritually stuck or uncertain about their next steps in their Faith. His teaching emphasizes both the simplicity and the depth of God's truths, urging believers to move beyond surface-level Christianity and into active, Spirit-led living.

Above all, Paul sees his life's purpose as a bridge builder—connecting biblical knowledge with everyday application, helping people go from simply attending church to truly *being* the Church. Through this book and others to come in the *Let's Get Back to Basics* series, he remains committed to his calling: to teach the uncompromised Word of God with clarity, conviction, and compassion.

STAY CONNECTED

PAUL M. BROMFIELD

I would love for you to stay connected with me as I continue my journey of ministry and writing. Follow, engage, and keep in touch through the following:

Email: For inquiries, or ministry updates, reach out via email:

PaulMBromfieldBooking@gmail.com

THANK YOU FOR READING!

I hope this book has blessed you, inspired you, and impacted your life. Your feedback is incredibly important, and I'd love to hear from you!

Leave a Review and 5-Star Rating

How to Leave a Review on Amazon

1. Go to the book's page on **Amazon** (search for the title or author).

2. Scroll down to the **Customer Reviews** section.

3. Click on **"Write a Customer Review."**

4. Select the number of stars and write your feedback.

5. Click **Submit**—and that's it!

Thank you for your support. Your feedback can help others find this book and experience the same life-changing message. May GOD continue to bless and guide you on your journey.

www.ingramcontent.com/pod-product-compliance
Lightning Source LLC
Chambersburg PA
CBHW071343150726
47997CB00002B/844